# Cambridge Elements ≡

Elements in Religion and Violence
edited by
James R. Lewis
*Wuhan University*
Margo Kitts
*Hawai'i Pacific University*

# VIOLENCE IN PACIFIC ISLANDER TRADITIONAL RELIGIONS

Garry Trompf
*University of Sydney*

CAMBRIDGE
UNIVERSITY PRESS

# CAMBRIDGE
## UNIVERSITY PRESS

University Printing House, Cambridge CB2 8BS, United Kingdom

One Liberty Plaza, 20th Floor, New York, NY 10006, USA

477 Williamstown Road, Port Melbourne, VIC 3207, Australia

314–321, 3rd Floor, Plot 3, Splendor Forum, Jasola District Centre,
New Delhi – 110025, India

103 Penang Road, #05–06/07, Visioncrest Commercial, Singapore 238467

Cambridge University Press is part of the University of Cambridge.

It furthers the University's mission by disseminating knowledge in the pursuit of
education, learning, and research at the highest international levels of excellence.

www.cambridge.org
Information on this title: www.cambridge.org/9781108731164
DOI: 10.1017/9781108584333

© Garry Trompf 2021

First published 2021

*A catalogue record for this publication is available from the British Library.*

ISBN 978-1-108-73116-4 Paperback
ISSN 2397-9496 (online)
ISSN 2514-3786 (print)

# Violence in Pacific Islander Traditional Religions

Elements in Religion and Violence

DOI: 10.1017/9781108584333

First published online: December 2021

Garry Trompf

*University of Sydney*

Author for correspondence: Garry Trompf, garry.trompf@sydney.edu.au

ABSTRACT: An Element on the role of violence in the traditional religions of the Pacific Islands (Melanesia, Micronesia and Polynesia) and on violent activity in islander religious life upon the opening of Oceania to the modern world. This work covers such issues as tribal warfare, sorcery and witchcraft, traditional punishment, and gender imbalance, and moves on to consider the continuation of old types of violence despite momentous socio-religious change.

KEYWORDS: violence, religion, payback, rebellion, rituals

ISBNs: 9781108731164 (PB), 9781108584333 (OC)

ISSNs: 2397-9496 (online), 2514-3786 (print)

# Contents

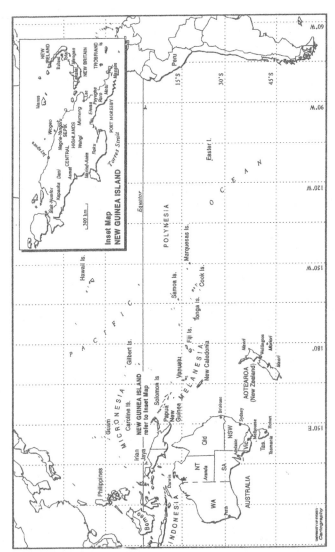

Figure 1 Map of the Pacific Islands

# 1 Background to the Study of Pacific Islander Life-Ways

The Pacific Ocean covers a third of the earth's surface, and its island world is scattered asymmetrically across vast tracts of water. While acknowledging continuing debate, convention among ethnographers since the eighteenth century has classified the peoples of the Pacific Islands into three human types that also generally present in three distinct far-flung regions (cf. Thomas 1989; Ryan 2002; and see Figure 1). Famously, these are:

*Melanesia* or 'the Black Islands' (islands of the blacks), spanning across the southwest Pacific from the western parts of the great island of New Guinea (the second-largest island non-continental land mass after Greenland) over to Fiji in the central Pacific (at least to Fiji's western half).

*Micronesia* or 'the Small Islands', many being coral atolls, basically stretching across the north-central Pacific from the Palau group (3,200 km from Japan) to Kiribati (2,140 km north of Fiji).

*Polynesia* or 'the Many Islands', constituting an enormous oceanic triangle from Hawai'i in the north to Rapanui or Easter Island to the east and Aotearoa or New Zealand to the south-west, the latter's south and north islands being the twelfth- and fourteenth-largest islands on Earth.

The peoples of these great islander groups share certain physical features in common, especially crinkly hair, but Melanesians are distinctive through their darker skin beside the relatively lighter-skinned Micronesian and Polynesian populations, a matter of interest when we find members of the two latter groupings showing up as traditional inhabitants of various coastal and offshore islands of Melanesia. Whereas the linguistic profile of Melanesia is highly complex, with over 800 heartland languages in various families along with over 300 Austronesian (or Malayo-Polynesian) tongues on the perimeter, both Micronesia and Polynesia form an overwhelmingly Austronesian language block (Wurm and Hattori 1981; Lynch 1998).

There are of course many islands lying on the Pacific's outermost 'Rim'. These include the Bering Strait Islands to the far north, for instance, or islands close to the western coasts of the Americas (such as the Santa Cruz Islands off California and the fabled Galapagos group off Peru), or islands close to eastern Australia (as in the Great Barrier Reef), and very significantly those off East and South-East Asia (from Japan, through Taiwan and the Philippines to Indonesia and Timor, especially west of the Wallace Line). But all these 'marginal spaces' can barely be discussed in this Element.

## *1.1 Pacific Island Religious Life in Broad Context*

Around a quarter of the discrete religions of the world are known from the Pacific Islands, the traditional ones all expectedly small-scale. Over millennia the peopling of the vast region of Oceania has involved extraordinary voyaging and daring exploration into formidable jungles and mountainous terrain. Reading the archaeology as we have it at the moment, black (now usually called 'Papuan') island discoverers were first into the southwest Pacific, the first signs of migration by boat being located off Bougainville Island and dated to 33,000± BP (Wickler 2001).[1] If 'Papuans' or 'Proto-Oceanic' peoples prevailed in the large islands extending beyond the Indonesian archipelago for some 50,000 years, and from before New Guinea and its outliers were geologically separated from the Australian mainland (7,000–6,500 BCE) (White and Connell 1982), a new cultural element has reached further around 3,000 years ago. In common convention it was distinctly 'neolithic' (compared to 'pre-neolithic') in technological achievement (Schmitz 1962: 124). Usually named Lapita after their distinctive pottery ware, Lapita traders were expert seafarers (*flor.* 3,500–500 BCE) whose route into the Pacific skirted the northern New Guinea Islands and reached Vanuatu, New Caledonia, Fiji, and even Tonga and Samoa (by 850–800 BCE). Recent DNA research connects them to the Taiwanese Indigenes, lighter-skinned Austronesian people who at first apparently kept separate from Melanesians, though the very far-reaching dispersal of peoples, north to Hawai'i, south to Aotearoa, came only after a mixing of types occurred (Spriggs 1996; Oxenham and Buckley 2016: 803–

---

[1]  Excavations being at Kilu, Buka, island of the darkest-skinned people on earth. Here we concede, though, the archaeological implications of intentional voyaging by boat to Flores Island and the continental shelf of Sahul tens of thousands of years before.

811; Skogland et al. 2016; cf. Kirch 2010).[2] Micronesia, however, had its own separate influxes from eastern Asia from around 1,500 BCE (some hold 3,000 years earlier), probably mostly from the Philippines, with subsequent aspects from the New Guinea Islands and beyond, while Polynesia's human spread was from the central Pacific itself. The Hawai'ian Islands and Aotearoa were reached during the thirteenth century CE (Rainbird 2004; Kirch 2017: 107–212; cf. Green 1967; Shutler 1975: 8–25, 100).

The renowned theory of Norwegian adventurer Thor Heyerdahl (1952: 156–170) that some Polynesians diffused from north-west America cannot stand (Trompf [1964] 2012), though his postulation of South American maritime input into Rapanui's prehistory may be retrievable, as also the claim that 'Polynesians' brought sweet potatoes into Oceania from the Americas (Heyerdahl and Ferdon 1961: 327; Golson 1981; Chapman and Gill 1997). Blood group and DNA lineages uniformly connect the Austronesian islanders to eastern Asia (Cox 2013). The material and cultural contribution of these Austronesians involved more refined Neolithic stone and vessel wares, as well as evidently more hierarchical societies, with paramount chiefs, even monarchs, and well-organized priesthoods and sacred architecture and sculpture. In the far east lie the great rows of Rapanui's giant *moai* statues of divinized chiefs overlooking ancestral lands, while much nearer the west lie Micronesian Pohnpe's *Soun Nan-leng* ('Reef of Heaven'), a mysterious 19-sq.-km stone-city-on-a-lagoon complex evidently serving as the royal cult center of the Saudeleur dynasty (*ca.* 1180–1630).[3] Among non-Austronesian 'Papuans' the material achievements were more basic, and a greater struggle pertained between 'equals' competing for leadership; indeed, Melanesian societies were generally acephalous, that is, without '*high*' chiefs or any 'royal social summit' (Swain and Trompf 1995: 7–8, 140–145; Anderson et al., 2009; Cochrane

[2] For the East Asian origins of Pacific Austronesians, work by Austrian archaeologist R. Heine-Geldern (1932) is seminal.

[3] Note Rainbird (2004: 314–315) on Leluh as well as Nan Madol (Pohnpe) and Phear (2007) on Babeldaob (Palau). For the archaeology of social stratification, see p. 9 on Roy Mata, and consider the usefully indicative variation and sequence of funeral practices in Palau archaeology (Fitzpatrick and Nelson 2008).

and Hunt 2018; cf. Sahlins 1963; Godelier and Strathern 1991; Kelly 1993). Out of the mysteries of 'Proto-Oceanic' sociolinguistic complexities in the highlands of New Guinea, though, the earliest-known garden cultivation occurred (8,000+ BCE, in Kuk, near Mount Hagen), reinforced by the Ipomoean (sweet potato) 'revolution' (Golson 2008, 2017).[4] Metalworking was only known at the very far west of the island world we are now going to examine (especially in western New Guinea's Vogelkop or Bird's Head region, due to expansion by the Muslim Sultan of Tidore from the eighteenth century). Despite some curious theories to the contrary, the traditional cultures, languages and religions of Oceania were barely touched by the pressures of the world's great religions until the first Christian (Jesuit) missions to Guam and the Marianas, Micronesia (from 1668).[5] Inaccessibility made parts of the New Guinea inland the slowest to experience outside impact, yet the greatest numbers of Pacific peoples were there.

This Element pretends to meet the challenge of exploring the relationship between a huge array of traditional religions and different patterns of human violence expressed over an enormous, unevenly populated span of terrestrial life. I admit to researching cultures of Oceania for more than sixty years, but this gives barely enough time to skim over the top of my own storehouse of field notes, interactions with fellow investigators and personal reading. I still plod along trying to piece together the oral and documented religious history of the great highland Wahgi Valley (with its ancient garden drains at Kuk) and wonder how many lifetimes would be necessary to comprehend a single small-scale Pacific culture-complex. I dare say there is some value in ageing scholars summarizing their findings, drawing out salience and formulating mature conclusions, and this will be me doing so within more concentrated limits than usual and on a very sensitive subject.

---

[4] The only contemporary interest in gently probing remnants of earlier religious strata (of supreme beings) and relating them to crop farming has come from Catholic theorists (partly affected by Wilhelm Schmidt and Adolf Jensen); see esp. T. Aerts (1998: 28–50); Mantovani (1984: 49–86).

[5] See Coella de la Rosa (2015). For a few signs of early Islam in Raja Ampat, as well as Moluccan–Biak Island trading voyaging and Biak wet-rice farming in the far west, see, for example, Kamma (1981: 92–93).

Because the rough population ratio in modern times seems to be around 16 to 1 in favor of the Melanesians over the Micronesians and Polynesians combined, more space will be devoted to the highly complex southwest Pacific scene (with which I am more familiar in any case), yet there is no neglecting both the historical significance and the achievements of more widely dispersed island peoples, especially the Polynesians.

For all the knowledge and careful consideration that should be brought to the topic at hand, might not a critical researcher of European heritage feel somewhat hesitant about probing violence in the stories of indigenous personages, even in long-past modes of existence, when it could fuel neocolonial and racially supremacist depreciation of marginalized peoples and disadvantaged groups? Why, how much in the history of classic European sociopolitical theory, deploying indigenous (including Pacific Islander) exemplars, has been devoted to express relief that the ways of savagery have been left behind for 'civilization'? The still-unexpunged stereotype of lives 'nasty, brutish and short', spent in hovels and filth, full of treachery, lies and vengeful bloodlust, is a patchwork of Western-documented 'native peoples' in their worst aspects, at the lowest stage before any 'progress' has begun (Trompf 1979: vol. 1: 15–25; vol. 2 [forthcoming, chs. 6–7]). In other words, it is an image of 'the violent-indigenous', basically the very same subject matter we address here! Of course the same tendencies to inferiorize have been appropriated and re-projected onto the very origins of religion in general, from the 'savage brutal clans of hunters', yet all too frequently with modern data on autochthonous, indigenous, small-scale traditional societies (in my youth so-called primitive peoples) called upon to fill in what the 'primary' or 'mother' or 'original' religion is supposed to have looked like (Anati 2020: 40–42; cf. Steinmetz 1892–1894). There are thorny issues to face and far too little space available, not just time, to do a proper job.

## 1.2 Dimensions of Violence and Religion in the Pacific Islands

Before addressing patterns of violence in Pacific Island religious histories, the whole question of the meanings put on violence and violent actions beckons immediate attention. For a start, intergroup (most often 'tribal') conflict was endemic to Pacific indigenous cultures, yet some scholars would consider the scale and technological level of its most serious outbursts to be 'feuding', not 'war'. Metal weaponry and guns were not used until serious contact with the outside world (from the sixteenth century), yet the flow-on of intergroup antagonisms using stone, bone and wooden weaponry into the post-lithic order make a feud/war distinction somewhat facile (Tefft and Reinhardt 1974: 154; Turney-High [1949] 1991; Otterbein 1994; cf. Collins 2008). More important points concern the effects of environments on the playing out of hostilities, so that groups utilizing traditional 'fighting grounds' or living at the borders of their language areas would engage in open-field warfare, whereas in rugged terrain, commonly slippery conditions or treacherous jungle, we find quick raids preferred to 'formalized contests', and, on large rivers and between islands, engagements can involve canoes, whether in larger-scale clashes or snap 'pirate' attacks (Jochim 1981: 32–63, 148–203).[6] We shall leave the details as to how 'religion' and 'violent collective assaults' interrelate to the following sections, but we should make clear initially that Pacific societies cultivated brave warriorhood among their young men (see Figure 2) and relied on the loyal support of women, who would most commonly, through exogamous rules, marry into their husband's people from potentially enemy groups (Keesing 1975: 13, 102).

A complex range or spectrum of violent acts across Pacific Island contexts also has to be acknowledged. 'Violence', we concede, is a cultural construct (Stewart and Strathern 2002: 1–14); but a certain globalizing 'common sense' (*sensus communis*), especially in internationalist formulations about specifically human transactions, allows us to proceed with sufficient confidence. Anticipating most readers' presumptions, it would be sensible to conceive a 'spectrum' between open physical homicide at one end and violent verbal acts at the other, with various possibilities in between. Thus we would place the actual killing of enemies in pitched battle or in quick raids or sudden encounters (of any enemy or stranger) towards one end of a yardstick, and quite apart from whether one group

[6] Note p. 198 of Jochim (1981) on border fighting – that is, between those of 'the same economy', even if their spoken tongues are not related.

Figure 2 Raiding party of Halia warriors, North Bougainville (*ca.* 1889). Photograph staged: R. H. R. Parkinson for *Album von Papúa Typen* (1894).

seeks to exterminate another or just occasionally pick off one or two of their foes. Academic quibbling might be had as to what best lies conceptually at the very extremity of open violence, because some analysts might choose 'murder' or a daring act of one individual to despatch another quickly in full public gaze, and questions of emotional ferocity, cruelty, cool ruthlessness, zeal for elimination and so on might come into estimates. At the other end of the scale would be verbal exchanges (aggressive words and gesticulations) or the percolating of malevolent rumours or accusations, which can bring two parties to the brink of emotionally charged physical jousting. It is possible that verbal altercations can stall physical fighting, even in shouting by leaders before a big battle, yet often close-encounter quarrelling can result in blows and thrusts, and of course in some cultures shame is felt like a mortal wound, demanding redress. Between the conceived 'polarities' lies a complex array of altercative possibilities. How to arrange them systematically will often depend on a scholar's choice of framing for educative or special hermeneutical purposes. There is no final or infallible approach. In my own work on revenge syndromes in Melanesia, I have naturally been interested in how kinds and degrees of violence reflect variations in group or personal propulsions to pay back others' perceived negative actions, threats or delicts – and thus in calculations and case-by-case or day-by-day reasoning lying behind action (Trompf 2008a).[7] Others have been interested in legitimacy: my late colleague Ronald Berndt (1962: 283, 414; 1964), for instance, defined war as '*justified* coercive action' by one unit over another 'to exact compensation or revenge for a real or imagined injury', with more stress on immediately knowing what is right (or that you are on the right side in an ongoing 'antagonistic game') than on probing cultural 'logics' of retribution (Berndt 1962: 283, 414; 1964). Other analysts again have psychoanalytic and sociobiological interests and thus explore the role of the unconscious or biological 'drives' (cf. Van der Dennen and Falger 1990: 149–271; Eibl-Eibesfelt 1991; Trompf 2005: 105–115, 133–143, 176–177, 215–224).

The archaeology of weapons in the island Pacific shows warfare and violent actions, and of course fortifications, definitely have a prehistory, yet with few exceptions the findings are as yet too scattered and limited to serve as anything more than a background to what we learn from oral and historical data. Weaponry is a consistent element in the record, yet of

---

[7] Note, in this approach, one cannot deduce that violence is always only for revenge or that revenge only involves physical violence. Group abstention from war, also, will discourage (yet does not rule out) the presence of other forms of violence (cf. Kelly 2000).

course weapons were also used for hunting, and we lack data from battle-grounds because instruments were mostly taken away (e.g., Bishop Museum 1892: Pt. II, 64–71; Golson 1959: 48–49, 55–58; Muke 1993; Otto et al. 2006: 75–88, 157–210 [including Brandt, Otto and Gosden]; cf. Knauft 1985). Earth- and stonework fortifications are better attested for Polynesia (Suggs 1960: 109–130; Green 1970; Daugherty 1979; Phillips 2001: 35–50, 105–158); there could have been more in Melanesia, but only isolated remnants of coral stone-walling have shown up (Dubois 1970: 55–60).[8] Because virtually everything in terms of belief gets lost to the four winds, it is tantalizing to know whether the digs and memories match sufficiently. A brilliant study of (largely open-air and stone-wall-enclosed) war temples in Hawai'i (especially at Kahikinui, Maui), together with a plotting of likely places of sanctuary, effectively uses corroborative evidence from oral traditions, including those on ritual human sacrifice at temple consecrations (Kolb and Dixon 2002: 520–521, 524). When the body of a chieftain was excavated on Eretoka Islet off Efate (Vanuatu), with his wife and twenty-two males and females buried as couples around him (*ca.* 1265 CE), we can only infer from local oral tradition that this was the great Roy Mata, who introduced the matrilineal kin system to an islander cluster and who was so honoured that men and women went willingly to their deaths to be with him in the thereafter. Whatever the precise circumstances, violence was done and revealed from beneath the sand (Bellwood 1978: 270–272; Garanger 1982).

Of meanings and actions in the spectrum between brutal homicides and vicious outcries, only minuscule bits survive archaeologically, and – as for almost all the material in this Element – reliance will be placed in subse-quent pages on oral memories, printed records, and my own extensive fieldwork experiences and habitation in Oceania. All sorts of ' in-between' configurations of violence will appear in the following pages. Typical for Pacific Islands cultures – but also for most other traditions the world round, as readers will immediately recognize – males have an 'apparent right' to discipline their wives by force (often also children and younger siblings),

---

[8] On defence-walling at Maré, Loyalty Islands (New Caledonia), *ca.* 250 CE, and deferring to oral tradition.

especially when issues of disloyalty and disobedience arise. And we are not to forget individual rivalries, so that *within* a group a one-on-one contest can occur, and whether through degree of bitterness or accident a death can follow. Such 'interpersonal violence' might be collateral damage in a dispute or perhaps amounting to 'an act of theft' (Younger 2015). Depending on the status of the perpetrator or the deceased, and if ferocious intent and culpability are plain, an intragroup killing would normally be rated as murder, usually punishable by death. Killing outsiders is forgivable (unless the target is a sensitive case) because it is equivalent on a small scale to 'serving one's nation', while scraps between personal enemies and smaller (lineage or clan) skirmishes within a wider tribe or grouping would be tolerated if non-lethal weapons were not used.

Mention of punishment already intimates that this Element will also have to account for violent sanctioning, especially executions, usually after decisions from the social apex (often monarchs and 'noble courts' in Polynesia, elders in Melanesia) have been made. Regulated measures of punitive violence will need some consideration (often as aspects of legal anthropology), with indigenous uses of imprisonment and prolonged torture virtually absent in traditional practice. Deployment of spirit powers (under names equivalent to magic, sorcery and witchcraft) can present as a form of punition if leaders call for it, yet, as we shall discover, how and when we can talk of violence with regard to the (negative) wielding of spirit power needs cautious analysis. There is also a rather messy range of special forms of 'violence' beckoning disentanglement, including socially accepted procedures bringing pain or temporary wounding to the body (tattooing, scarification etc.) or ambiguous or rejected acts (rape, unfriendly death-rites, suicide etc.). Mock violence and belligerence can form part of ceremonies with potential or former enemies, warning against treacherous behaviour. As we proceed, details as to how conflict is contained or halted will sometimes be noted, although (as we confess from time to time as well) the task of writing this Element carries the unfortunate side effect of neglecting peaceful energies.

Violent actions in Pacific Islander religions are not only between humans but include the killing of animals – sometimes spectacularly, as in the mass ceremonial slaughter of pigs. We can generally distinguish despatches in hunting (or the elimination of nearby fauna that has become dangerous, such as wild boars or crocodiles) and the sacrificing of creatures in ritual or relationship-bonding contexts. In various indigenous contexts, plants can be treated as the equivalent of humans (rooted out and beheaded, perhaps apologetically!), with slashing and burning of forest for garden grounds carrying the sense of destructiveness or sacrifice. Inert objects taken to be charged with spirit power (effigies, masks etc.) can be discarded when no longer destroyed to start a new cycle of things or out of revenge against enemies – usually not without fear of occult consequences. In the Islands, stones and wood obstructing one's way can be hit with unapologetic anger: it is not as if every part of the environment is 'animated', but special parts of it are; as a whole, one's land is revered, and wild places contain spiritual dangers that violent deeds cannot withstand.

What of 'religion'? To clarify the Element's approach at the onset, traditional religion in general and each in particular is taken seriously, without inclination to reduce it as in some sense insufficient or just betraying 'religious manifestations' as 'shamanism, animism and totemism' (Anati 2020: 41, cf. Keesing 1982: 1–12 setting a high standard). This integrity holds true even while we will find that, though only a select few custodians or specialists hold the means to conceptualize the world view and overall praxis of a particular culturo-linguistic complex, trained researchers can readily intuit or apprehend it as a traditional religion (note Brunton 1980). By now it will be obvious that 'religions' in this Element are considered to be 'total life-ways', or complex entwinings of received outlooks and customary behaviour. And I have not changed my previous definition of religion as 'those concerns that most dominate people's acts, reasonings and feelings because they understand their cosmos to be affected by living agencies, spirit-beings, and other non-human forces' that can be made 'subject to human influence' (Trompf 2008a: xvi). Whatever tradition-related actions people carry out under the weight of this view of things are religious actions. In what I deem to be inveterately 'martial' or 'warrior' societies' of the Pacific, violent deeds are integral to religious life: they are so often ritualized, carried out because of expectations from the spirit world, and in accordance with ancestral laws taken as inviolable. This Element, then, is patently about religions expressing themselves in violence, not about violence in forms or examples attached to different and named cultures, as if we forever thereafter have to pinpoint specifically religious factors generating it. In other writings I have discussed how complexes of thought and action tending towards hostility get connected by 'local logic' to more concessive modes and form the means by which events in everyday life are explained in consensus ways. I have not denied, moreover, that violent acts can present as most important events of salvation – saving from attack, capture, cannibalism or spiritual threat – offering tangible benefits without the spiritualization of *Erlösung* found in more widely spread, more honoured religions. In their typical concern for the basics of survival, however – for relief from enemies or victory over them, and bounty of their struggles in awkward environments – traditional religions expose what has probably been the longest-lasting substance of 'religion in general', the need to secure succour, visible success or 'blessing' in this life, as well as the prospect of more of it in the hereafter. This is the yearning that has propelled the emergence of larger social unities and fuelled territorial expansions that then laid the bases for empires (starting with the Akkadians from *ca.* 2300 BCE) that are always dependent on violent coercion. And no matter how hard those in the famous traditions have sought to overcome or tame them, or questing souls have wanted us to think more deeply, these persistent energies for violent actions simply will not be wished away and are re-manifested to this day even where formal religion withers under secularity's desert sun; indeed, they can very easily undermine and overtake the highest ideals (Trompf 1988; 2017: 16–17). These recurrent pulsations are problematic, then, and by historical inference they 'make religion a problem', because they look to go back to basic struggles for survival in a world of more-or-less equally competing and as yet unsubjugated forces. By typical moves of lateral thinking, they render Pacific Islanders' almost ubiquitously warriorhood religions[9] also problematical and in turn generate a methodological *problématique* for academic investigators like me.

---

[9] For possible deep-forest 'pygmy high forest' and 'non-sedentary' exceptions, see, for example, Numazawa (1965) (barely accessible Kobon, PNG Eastern highlands) and Trompf (1986: 23–24) (extinct, Zia-related Seragi, PNG Papuan highlands).

Modern critical scholarship presumes a solid grip on objectivity, but with issues of both religion and violence the handhold can rather quickly turn slippery. It has been a permission in modern social studies that one can study compartments of human livelihood, and thus, especially when it comes to ethnographic, ethnological, ethnohistorical or anthropological studies, one can find published research focused on or dividing up facets of socio-cultural existence (that in turn relate to sub-disciplines attending to them). Thus we find anthropologies of conflict and war; political and organizational anthropology; social anthropology or kinship studies; subsistence or economic anthropology and studies of material culture; social and ethno-psychology; legal anthropology; and so on. On reflection, though, in apprehending the discrete small-scale affairs of 'first' or 'native' peoples covered in this Element, we are dealing with 'whole ways of life'. And though terms such as 'population', 'human group', 'shared language', 'society', 'culture' and 'totality' have their own value encapsulating these unities, 'tradition', 'customary ways' and above all 'indigenous religion' give them full body, especially because such 'encompassing outlooks' stand even when social fracturing is serious and the actual sociology of cultural knowledge very unordered and uneven (across age and gender). One admittedly comes across 'religious anthropology', as that which concentrates on 'leading cosmic beliefs' and 'key collective rituals', yet this will only produce very misleading results when 'the religious', 'the spiritual', the 'cosmically received', or outlooks and actions in the presence of the ancestors and spirit-beings permeate all existence. A cautious historical awareness is also called for when conceptual and formulaic recognitions of 'primitive', 'primal', 'tribal' or 'traditional religion' grew within European discourse, and out of missionary and colonial encounters, as an interpretative series of 'inventions' looking less and less depreciative (Ranger 1992: 253–254; Bielo 2015). In the following pages I read traditional Pacific Islander religions as complete ways of being, and for that reason I approach expressions of violence as intrinsic to them while hardly exhausting their intricacies, synergies and possibilities. That means they present the challenge to respect and tackle their problematical aspects.

This Element must necessarily engage in different academic disciplines (as in the case of most of my writings). My chosen fields of study – the History of Ideas, Studies in Religion, and Peace and Conflict Studies – are already multidisciplinary, but it will be obvious how much I rely on a wide range of social scientific researchers, especially in Anthropology (cf. Ralph 2012; Lee 2019). As an interdisciplinary scholar, though, I am hardly unconcerned with practical issues, especially since I hold an adjunct professorship in Peace and Conflict Studies. Most historians and social scientists can enjoy a certain comfort from their would-be objectivism in just describing what they uncover, but various scholars, including myself, concern themselves with the management of practical problems in societies. Addressing 'religion and violence', of all things, and in the Pacific Islands, of all places, where life matters are very basic existentially, fairly impels commitment to high idealism – peace with justice, love as unconquerable goodwill, implacable quest for truth, as I have already disclosed them for myself (Trompf 2011: 124b) – immediately inviting charges of bias. My value orientations may sound very Quaker-like, squaring with the huge fait accompli of Christian missionary and national church endeavours to 'transform the old warrior spirit into positive channels', and may appear as abetting a rampant process secularists or defenders of tradition find irksome (Trompf 2012).[10] This Element, nonetheless, together with works I admire by scholars of varied persuasions anxious to diminish levels of violence (Strathern and Stewart 2011; Dinnen and Ley 2013; Rankine et al. 2015), will reflect my dual quest for accurate documentation yet aversion to human maltreatments, and, even if there is irritatingly little space here to discuss non- or other-than-violent phenomena, my pursuit of more just social and socio-environmental arrangements will inevitably show. The whole subject itself is

[10] Here noting that church pacification work has broadly accorded with colonial, neocolonial and postcolonial policies to secure public order. For sorting out questions of friction between anthropological objectivism and commitment to spiritually generated ideals, turn to works by, see Larsen (2014) on E. Evans-Pritchard, M. Douglas, and E. and V. Turner.

enormous, of course, not just contentious, and I remain humbled by it: but somehow I have retained fire in the belly to complete the job.

These introductory observations are followed in the main body of the text by detailing the enmeshing of Pacific Islander religions and patterns of violence. Our first approach (Section 2.2) will be synchronic, overviewing the highly complex data on Melanesia, addressing ethos, warrior initiation, warfare, punishment, sacrifice, and issues of sorcery and witchcraft in turn. Our second approach, diachronically and historically oriented (Section 2.3), will give more space to Polynesia and the wider Pacific, under the rubrics of warfare and ethos.

# 2 Violence and Traditional Religions

Since there are almost 1,400 traditional languages and cultures in the Pacific Island world under scrutiny, the reader is at the mercy of invidious circumstances: too much material to distil; too much data to absorb; too much evidence lost; very many different perspectives already affecting the presentation of individual ethnographies; and the problem of having to trust the present author in trying to provide a useful synoptic account (albeit from personal research starting in 1958). Presuming the first two difficulties to be obvious, I will make a few cursory observations about what is lost, about the contest of interpretative stances and about the principles governing my own approach.

## 2.1 Preliminary Questions of Perspective

Regarding losses of information, only a small minority of cultures remain who practise traditional warfare (all in isolated parts of Melanesia), and the custodians of detail about traditional methods and rationales for fighting or uses of violence are dying off rapidly without their stories being passed down or recorded. The Pacific has become mostly 'pacified' through external pressures: the prevailing ethos of proud male warriorhood has given way to the combined, if not perfectly concordant, influences of church and government. Missions have long called for peaceful existence, and both colonial and new-national institutions have always required law-abiding and 'civilized' activity (Rodman and Cooper 1983). The presumption behind this Element, of course, is that we need not be drawn into very long-term issues. We are not about to prove small-scale island societies were at war or significantly violent through prehistoric times (over the forty-eight millennia of slow inhabitancy), as if we have to discount 'the myth of the peaceful savage', nor reconcile ourselves sociobiologically to human violence as 'anchored in survival' from the start, nor wait for sufficient-enough indications of weaponry from Paleolithic to pre-contact times (cf. Keeley 1996: 25–70, 99–142; Thayer 2004; 268 et passim; Trompf 2005: 215–224). In any case, individual 'digs' may not happen to be in spots where fighting artefacts are likely to show up: the most important archaeological site of the Oceanic region, Kuk swamp in the central New Guinea Highlands, where human horticulture may have had its beginning 10,000 years ago, has actually yielded few weapons. More to the point of this study is that a particular style of weaponry has formed a mark of identity for most individual Pacific cultures, by look, chosen materials, carving, serrations, colouring and so on. (Golson 2017: 368; cf. Muke 1993; Oliver 2002: 53–60; Rossi 2018: 119–132).[11] If we have these leftover indicators, whether from collectors or through archaeology, we are indeed their lucky possessors. Missionaries could organize the symbolic burning of stacked spears or receive relinquished spirit stones used for martial empowerment and sorcery to smash them symbolically, as markers of the new peace. Many relevant objects in wickerwork or decorated by feathers, confiscated or given away to outsiders, have unfortunately never reached places where they can be best preserved for posterity (e.g., Dupeyrat 1964: Pettifer and Bradley 1990: 61; King 2011).[12] But distinctive physical artifices of violence

---

[11] On continuity of style, note how sacred adzes on Tikopia (a Polynesian outlier), the dark ones inter alia used in killer magic against thieves, remained the same recognizable shape even when metal blades replaced shell or stone (Firth 1959: 149–156).

[12] For alleged cases of wanton cultural destruction by missionaries, see for Bishop Joseph Loerks (on his white charger) in the East Sepik (New Guinea) (Tuzin 1997: 20) (vehemently against such 'cultural vandalism'); compare with Huber (1987: 115–117) (more contextual); and for Fr Honoré Laval on Mangareva and

were simply endemic to the region, and styles were commonly 'earmarked' when traditional cultures came in contact with the outside world.

Apropos diverging perspectives, readers would have already expected a collision of views between those (especially on-the-ground missionaries and officials) who are implacably opposed to every sign of tribal feuding and those idealists who consider indigenous people should be left untouched, to work things out for themselves. As for anthropological accounts of warfare, interestingly they can vary in their detailing, from basic neglect to main focus. A fieldworker in a place where mission talk has already instilled relative peace can be satisfied with writing what he observes and does not have to bother with what is not there any more. Even the great pioneering Bronislaw Malinowski could feel personally secure through prior Methodist presence on the Trobriand Islands (Island Papua) and treated his brief consideration of 'regular fighting' in token fashion, clearly idealizing its order and honour (Malinowski 1920; cf. 1926: 71–125). Where traditional fighting still goes on, well nigh exclusively in isolated uplands of Melanesia's main New Guinea island, it will be a major subject of investigation, and the more so because it is a fast-passing side to traditional life, paradoxically precious and worth preserving in ethnography before being lost forever.[13]

That Melanesian regions, both thick with jungle and the last to be 'contacted', retain pockets of traditional warfare relates to another matter of scholarly debate over historico-temporal perspectives. With much earlier contact elsewhere, the general impression has stuck that great conquering

the Gambiers (French Polynesia) as unbalanced zealot, see Eskridge (1931: 175–183) ('mad priest'); compare with Jedin (1971: vol. 2, 243) ('autonomous theocracy', Laval recording past customs).

[13] Note the use of the problematic terminology 'unique laboratory' of conflict data in 'Precontact Oceania' by Younger (2015: 2). Continuing traditional tribal fighting on the New Guinea mainland, fighting can be found in small pockets among outlying Lani or Ilaga Dani (the largest language grouping of the West Papuan/Irian highlands) and in isolated north-western Southern Highlands and near the Schrader Ranges, Papua New Guinea. Many new forms of tribal fighting have erupted with access to non-traditional weaponry (as discussed later and in a companion Element, *Violence and Religious Change in the Pacific Islands*).

and colonizing external powers – from the sporadic Chamorro Wars on Micronesia's northern Marianas in the late seventeenth century (1668 to 1699) (Hezel 2015: 19–44) to the last of the Maori wars (Aotearoa/New Zealand) (ending 1872) (Cowan and Hasselberg [1922] 1983) – brought on fighting mentalities previously unknown among relatively 'peace-loving', 'gender-equalizing' peoples of Micronesia and Polynesia (cf. Keeley 1996: 3–24; Linnekin 1997). Post- and anti-colonial attitudes bolster this characterization, because, in the tourist-attractive, scattered-island parts of Oceania, unless one digs for the manuscripts, it is hard to believe islanders would be senseless enough to maraud each other in reef-bound idyllic spaces (Salzman 1990: 34; Wirihana and Smith 2014). Marxist theorists generally make missionaries complicit in colonial enterprises and remain suspicious of any very early records of war as constructions to legitimize conversion. And there remains the theory that introduced disease not only decimated Pacific Island populations (in a complicated mainly-nineteenth-century story involving shipwreck survivors, castaways, beachcombers and traders, besides missionaries and government personnel) but also caused unprecedented conflict (Rivers 1922; Lambert 1934; Moorehead 1966: 8–97; Sand 2000: 53–63). Certainly, as on Malekula (New Hebrides/Vanuatu), depopulation sometimes owed much more to tribal war with firearms than to disease (Layard 1942: 42–43, 477–487); and obviously individual gun-toting Europeans, who backed one group against another, could cause decimation (as in the striking case of sandalwood seeker Charles Savage, who became warrior and chief on Fiji's fortress islet of Bau, 1808–1813) (Campbell 1980). Yet we also learn how new sicknesses, carried from coastal trading points deep inland into many infection-vulnerable pockets, were blamed on enemy sorcery, not on unknown germs, creating more fearful attention to one traditional pretext for war than previously.[14] Debates though there may be, we learn that even hints of first contact (such as the fleeting visit of a European ship in one bay, the *Cumberland* at

---

[14]  These arguments about sorcery accusation were first persistently put in the teaching of my colleague the late Edgar Waters, with relevant medical research pointing in the same direction; see inter alia Jenkins et al. (1989).

Rarotonga in 1814, for instance) could seriously reignite intra-island conflict from sheer jealousy that one tribe was visited and not another.[15]

The facts remain: indicators of traditional aggressiveness are purveyed across the whole Pacific Island world. Where the balance of alliances was tight, the desire to eliminate enemies could still be accepted as a collective purpose (as among the famed Dugum Dani, Baliem Valley, West Papua) (Gardner and Heider 1969), and there were genuine (if failing) attempts to exterminate foes completely – the Tolai against the Baining (on New Britain, New Guinea Islands, with enslavement also involved) and the Bena Bena against the Asaro (New Guinea Eastern Highlands), for key examples (Trompf 2008a: 45, 47) – and in the wider Pacific we find the dreaded Tautuans of Tongareva (Penryhn Is.), who efficiently combined killing with tight subjection (Hiroa/Buck 1932: 55–56). This is not to forget, either (even if often enough done), that there were traditional imperial conquests (and collective subjugations in consequence) long before wider-world impacts (Swain and Trompf 1995: 7–8). Relying on fear of their powerful and sanctioning magicians, Yap (or more particularly the Gagil grouping on it) took strong control of scattered western Micronesian atolls, especially from *ca.* 1700 to 1850, expropriating large stones from the volcanic islands of Palau (Belau) to the south-west for their cumbersome money system and receiving tribute in coconut oil, sennit, pandanus sails and mats from such islands as Ulithi, Woleai and Ifaluk to the east in a graded system of dependency (Lessa 1950). Still farther spread than the Yapese 'empire' were those of Samoa and Tonga, as successive inter-island dominions. Tonga was at its strongest through the sixteenth and seventeenth centuries, with takeover and weak colonization reaching as far west as the Isle of Pines (near the southern tip of the New Caledonian mainland), as far north as Wallis, and into eastern Fiji, the Tongans wisely stopping at Viwa in a close face-off with those feared cannibals of Bau (Scarr 2013: 48–52). Such empires, to which we can add sub-Incan maritime incursions into the Galapagos and Rapanui (Easter Is.) (Moseley 1975: 39–90), are difficult to place for not fitting prior theory – though some Marxists, as least, read them as

---

[15] The case is recorded in a MS held by the Polynesian Society, University of Auckland, by Maretu, "Rarotongan History" (Wellington, 1871), 2, 8(a)–9(a), 15–22, 39, 134.

an 'Asiatic mode of production' (Wittfogel 1981: 241).[16] But they are part of the broad picture I seek to paint in this Element.

Concerning my own position, given my professional commitments to peacemaking (Ionesov and Trompf 2022), learned by hard experience and affecting my theoretical position (see Section 1.2), I will need to arrive at a workable balance between respect towards others and holding by one's own values. In a survey work like this, questions will naturally arise as to whether one can encapsulate *Weltanschauungen* held by human groups responsibly and faithfully enough (taking into account, for example, differing attitudes towards violence between males and females). The ideal is to get representations straight, to do justice to religious world views even though validations and enactments of violence are built into them. One may acknowledge how easy it can be to enter into the spirit of things and fall into a fighter's mode of thinking and responding – the 'retributive logic' of possessing the reasons for taking revenge with your war group, a crucial component of traditional Pacific Islander traditional religions. On the other hand, there is an art to keeping one's distance as a scholar. While one can see why some peoples can glory in past victories, indeed in past island empires, and also appreciate that reputed social theorists around the globe have gauged the greatness of nations on their willingness to accept bloody conflict (e.g., Lasaulx 1854: 79–88; Murray 1928: 9, 15, 18; with Crook 2003), there is good reason to recognize that, over the last two centuries, Pacific Islanders have been increasingly happy to leave the artifices of traditional brutality behind – and thus to write things up more out of this realization than from any ready celebration of old vitalities.

In what follows, the prior promise shall be fulfilled to approach the relevant material first synchronically (Section 2.2), looking at the massive documentation of violence and religion found especially in anthropological writing; and then diachronically or historically (Section 2.3), dividing our attention between Melanesia and wider Oceania, especially Polynesia, with a greater usage of old records and oral historical evidence.

---

[16] In Chief Malopa'upo Isaia (1999: esp. 35) and Taumoefolau (2012) we find fulsome indigenous revivals of enthusiasm over Samoa's and Tonga's successive expansions (with the alleged transition between the two *ca.* 950 CE).

## 2.2 A Synchronic Approach

An ethnographer of any particular culture can opt to document only what pertains *presently*, thus examining a society's structures and functioning parts 'across the board' from a synchronic perspective. In not considering what is past or changing, it is viable and useful to provide a non-historical orientation to Oceanic religions that discerns *cultural components* most regularly relevant for an investigation, in our case interconnections between world views and violence. Thus we could say, though we lack many bits and pieces of information, that Pacific societies each have a 'general repertory' of attitudes and actions that a researcher may expect, despite the need to fill out special details and eccentricities, to reveal 'religiosity' and 'violence' to be integrally or interdependently expressed (see Knauft 1999: 89–156; Trompf 2006: 693–694). Indeed, by this means, 'warrior religion' or 'martial social orders' can be better detected in their worldwide manifestations. Gone should be the days when ethnographers can arbitrarily compartmentalize war and religion or means of violence and *Weltanschauungen* in traditional societies, or even for that matter between 'the religious' and 'the economic', because they are utterly intertwined within each life-way. With few exceptions, Pacific Island children were born into miniature worlds in which violent conflict was the stuff of everyday existence and the art of living was to learn the ropes of staying alive in a tense context (certainly not in the paradisiacal Pacific Island state of Western dreams!).

Pacific environments, for a start, were not without dangers lying outside difficult human relations. There were the hard realities of isolated (and premodern) conditions, of course, from treacherous weather and seas to spiking sago palms to crocodile attacks, from volcanic eruptions to blight, from natal fatalities to falls from coconut palms. But the cosmos was also traditionally understood to be inhabited by dangerous or unpredictable spirit forces. Beyond the safest surrounds (the house clusters of one's childhood) or locations of persons (at home, in the gardens, on excursions) (e.g., Biersack 1995: 1–54 on PNG highland groups), or beyond what Peter Lawrence (1984: 8–60, 126–160) has described for the Madang hinterland Garia (PNG) as one's 'security circle' (of immediate family, extended family [typically agnates] and [affine] relatives by marriages), there were unsafe places inhabited by other-than-ordinary humans. We should start our investigations with Melanesians, because their cosmic orientations in spatial terms were typically 'horizontal' – generally towards the horizon – whereas Micronesian and Polynesian cosmologies, as we shall see, are recognizably more 'vertical' – sky/heaven above; earth in the middle; depths/underworld below.

## 2.2.1 Melanesia

### 2.2.1.1 *Ethos*

Spiritual uncertainty and danger in characteristic Melanesian outlooks lay in low-lying murky swamps or on mountain-heights frequented by place spirits (Tok Pisin: *masalai*), sometimes connected to dangerous creatures like snakes. The Papuan Highland Fuyughe, for instance, hold each eerie mountaintop plateau overlooking their valleys to be ruled by a *sila*, a python-connected spirit who kills all daring to make a crossing (Trompf 2004: 13). In most Melanesian settlements, ghosts not released to the spirit-world are commonly thought to be heard at night from the forest, unnervingly, and danger awaits those encountering them on some less-used track (Chowning 1975: 84). We actually hear of 'war ghosts (*agalimae*)' being worshipped in Malo (North Malaita, Solomon Islands), their prowess celebrated in song for arriving far back as outsiders to bring 'the beginning of war' (Ivens 1930: 141–147), while in other quarters the first use of effective weapons for fighting was credited to some honoured culture hero, such as Kilibob or Manup of the Madang Island peoples (off the New Guinea coast), who in variant accounts also established the war god in mythic time (Pech 1991). I remember spending a pleasant morning in 1974 (1,500 meters up in the central New Guinea Highlands) with a Wahgi 'magician'-specialist, who explained how he diagnosed the trouble or sickness that could befall any of his clients if they had disturbed (by hunting or fighting beyond safe settlements, etc.) any of at least sixteen major 'wild spirits' (*kangekes*) and how much he charged (usually in pigs) for a cure (Trompf 2008a: 138–139). Over a decade earlier, my late colleague, Ralph Bulmer, one of the great classificatory ethnobiologists of all time, tried translating all the different classes he could find among the Kyaka Enga (far-western New Highlands) of such 'nasties' that interfered with the active life: nature demons, forest spirits (often equated with ancestral ghosts), 'the "stranger" ghost' and 'the female forest spirit', cannibal ogres, tree spirits, echoes, snails, and some animals such as the potentially inimical *raleya* lizard or the 'Black Chat' omen bird and so on (Bulmer 1965: 135–136). For Enga groupings in general (making up the largest autochthonous language block in the Pacific), life is a war on angry ghost-creatures (who bring trouble and sickness), likened to a war on enemies: myths warn of and ratify this, and rituals are carried out for protection from looming sky-beings (Brennan 1977: 14–18, 56 n. 49; cf. 27–31, 36–45). The Kyaka cult ground, instructively, is called *imbwunda* ('house of hate') (Bulmer 1962: 201). The Melanesians' non-human environment, indeed, is alive with violent potential.

We present this material because Indigenes have grown up with a sense of inhabiting *their land*, and in every known case it is accepted as possessing sacred associations. But it follows that territory taken to belong to one's group is *shared* by non-humans: it has spirits belonging within it, and narratives are kept about their separate claims over it. In various legends we hear of animals, or more often than not serpents, able to take human form and disturb human relationships (killing their spouses or children), but it is often in these spirit-beings' flight, after being discovered for their acts, that their movements from one named place to another help mark out the landscape familiar to listeners of myth and legend. Place is not human-named but an already god- or spirit-originated layout, often as a result of some surreptitious killing that has to happen for the known cosmos to 'occur' (Z'graggen 1995; Lohmann 2019; cf. Jensen 1951 for background). Sometimes the legendary fleeing-traveller is victim, as Yarong – the fertility spirit with 'all kinds of food hanging as part of her skin', honoured by the Bargam (Madang coast) – who runs across 'the known land' from her wild-cannibal husband Saimor, after he eats her child (Ramram in Trompf 2008b: 28–29). The constant threat of stronger man over weaker woman is also implied here. The renowned culture hero Manarmakeri, the route of whose precarious voyaging surprisingly pinpoints the *topoi* of the Biak-Numfor region (island West Papua), was also first a rejected victim, in his guise of a scabrous old man (again with an extra implication that the old are not to be maltreated) (Thimme 1977: 21–24). Sometimes, legends portray the tilling of gardens and their produce as thwarted by prior spirits, the annoying *Mapou* ('short people') in Matangkor lore (Baluan Island, Manus group, New Guinea Islands), for instance, having to be attacked by surprise and eliminated, in stories probably reflecting takeover (the diminution of earlier inhabitants' statures being a common feature in Pacific Island tales) (Kasau in Trompf 2008b: 30–31; cf. Luomala 1951). The elements of violence purveyed in story were inculcated in child-rearing, localized education and common ethos.

Pondering the last illustration, of course, it can hardly be assumed that most people upon 'contact' had always been in the locations first documented for them. Many are those orally preserved memories of fissures and resultant migrations, with groups buffeted by other groups having to win for themselves their 'places in the sun' (Trompf 2017). Many are the heroic stories of single women escaping from a massacre with a baby and thereafter starting a new hamlet, as I began to learn on my first Melanesian field trip among the Motu (coastal Papua, in 1972), to take in the legendary founding of Taurama village, symbolically opposite the bluff where the Motuan culture hero Edai Siabo received 'cosmic secrets' from under the waters about how to make riches by daring trade voyaging, and ironically right next to the Murray barracks, a fixture of Australian colonial control (cf. Oram 1968; Lacey 1985: 98–99). A much more populous lot, such as the Huli (Southern Highlands, Papua), might sing an old song 'We Are a [Whole] People!' because the sun will 'rise and stay' over their large territory most of the day and passes so quickly over neighbouring peoples! But such overall consolidation belies the fact that their smaller 'cognatic allegiances' have also fought strenuously with one another, some far less successfully than others (Swain and Trompf 1995: 123; cf. Glasse 1968). Myth, legend and fireside talk of heroic deeds, then, all make up crucial conditioning atmospheres of prevenient struggles that interrelate the proud or notorious exertions of spirits, ancestors and the ordinary living. Dwelling or voyaging close to where souls will proceed at death brings with it a deeper sense of one's place-of-belonging near enough to those who lived and died bravely (as for Trobrianders) (Ketobwau 1994, ahead of Mosko 2017). Because the daily round is lived in a communing of the living seen and the living unseen, the dead are always honoured by leaving scraps after each meal, coming as vermin quietly come to take what they need (Jaua, an Orokaiva grouping, coastal northern Papua) (Trompf 2008a: 120). Ancestral land itself can be justifiably alienated, gifted to an allied lineage that saved the day in a feud (Arapesh, near coastal New Guinea) (Narokobi 1983: 85). On the other hand, there was always the danger of offending the dead or reckoning with vindictive 'ghost-relatives', whose anger can cause a child to fall sick (Wahgi) (Trompf 2008a: 134) or who can invisibly and poisonously spit into food if too many people prepare it (Eastern Toaripi, Papuan Gulf) (Eri 1970: 19).

In Melanesia, if we now can concentrate more on the expectations put upon members of small-scale warriorhood cultures, matters come to a head for the young in initiatory procedures, as preparation to participate in the arts of cooperation that ensure both security and prowess. In the layout of hamlet building, children soon learnt the difference between ordinary dwellings (family houses mostly occupied by women and children) and places which they would not approach without permission. The large men's house, a chief's house or a great cult house that combined cultic and men's activities were places forbidden to children's entrance yet awesomely visible. Mothers' talk of initiations in connection with such places created a prolonged sense of anticipation. Among the Ilahita Arapesh (east Sepik River plains), the ominous knotted rope dangling over the great highly painted façade of the spirit house (*haus tambaran*) indicated the demands and punished victims of Nggwal, a kind of 'Cyclopean' embodiment of all spirits, frighteningly warning against misbehaviour (Tuzin 1974: 324). A tabued pole, centrally placed in the 'piazza' of Mekeo villages and opposite the imposing chiefs' house (hinterland Papua), was not to be touched by anyone, infants included, and even doing so inadvertently would incur immediate execution. If any pre-initiated child was taken to a tribal border, fixtures would usually be there to alert leavers as well as visitors, effigies of the vacant-staring, long-earlobed war god Tiola being set up as boundary-markers by the powerful Roviana (of New Georgia, western Solomon Islands).[17] Across the board, young boys would be encouraged to take on each other with pointed sticks or small stones and to jeer whenever real

---

[17] Using my Fieldnotes 1985 (for Aipiana, Mekeo) and 1980 (Roviana Lagoon, New Georgia); cf. Trompf (2004b: [pl. 3]).

enemy groups were mentioned in conversation, story or acted farce, while in a few cultures boys had to face pre-initiatory, painful, prepubescent rites of circumcision (see Dark 1974: 15, 18, 40, 48 and figs. 92–93 for the Kilenge, West New Britain; and Gewertz 1983: 286–295 on Chambri Lakes). Formal initiation, however, constituted the crucial means of social belonging or membership in a warrior world.

One has to remember that children growing up, playing and in friendly enough relations with each other were assessed by elders to be ready for initiation as a cohort (say around ten boys), drawn out of lineages across a clan (even a whole tribe of allied clans). This was typically done, however, under the supervision of uncles, most often paternal (the father's brother) but also involving maternal or classificatory uncles, who generally did not reside where a child was brought up but had to witness, if not involve themselves in, the initiation itself. Although kinship systems varied, children usually grew up under the care of their mother as a woman who had married into a clan exogamously (from another tribe), who thus lived with her husband's people, and who (in an arena of shifting alliances, often made through marriages) had to prove her loyalty, usually among a circle of older women 'strangers' as the prior custodians of local female rules.[18] A woman's children constituted the closest relationship of her life. Generally speaking, husbands did not see that much of their wives (often enough possessing more than one), nor did they dwell continuously with them in 'family houses'; and women were impregnated most often away from dwelling areas (at opportune times in gardens or in the nearby 'bush'). Come initiations, women would not like the prospect of relinquishing the sons they nurtured (or children they helped rear or adopted), and mothers often made known their complaints jointly, even if girls were left and had to be prepared for their own *rites de passage* into womanhood.

We generalize here as best we can, of course, and in the complexity of so many cultures, different conditions applied. A young Asaro boy (Eastern New Guinea Highlands) would have to know different variations of his language depending on which relative or individual he encountered,

---

[18] For kinship variations in Melanesia, esp. Benedict (1935: 94–98); and classificatory and 'phratry' relationships, e.g , Bateson (1958: 94–95, 305).

especially during trade exchanges forged along affinal lines (or because of marriage connections), and in a culture where friends would greet by grasping each other's testicles or where women rub one another's upper leg, you would want to learn early to avoid making a reprehensible move (Read 1966: 95–140). In some cases of endogamous marriage relations, as within a *susu* or great marriage circle of the Massim (eastern and island Papua), the women can sometimes be found larger in stature than many men, with some power in military affairs and the first to teach their sons fighting skills (cf. Young 1983). Across the region, young prepubescent boys were encouraged to be in the company of men to learn fighting skills and to scrap with other boys using blunt arrows (Poignant 1972: 22–260). Among the western (Ilaga) Dani in the West Papuan highlands, it would not be an unexpected sight to see young boys bouncing along behind a fighting party (see Figure 3), as they leave to or return from battle, their mothers carrying extra weapons for their fathers (Mitton 1983: 87–88).

## 2.2.1.2 Initiation

Male initiation is a subject made complex by the fact that certain societies offer higher grades of initiatory rites through further stages of the life cycle, but well-nigh uniformly across Melanesia primary ceremonies were introductions into both adult life and warrior responsibility. Such primary initiation often involved a psychological wrenching of boys from their mothers, who vocally lamented the rupture, when supervising uncles herded a selected cluster of initiands into seclusion, often first to a special fenced-off precinct or into a men's house. The preface to proceedings over the months of instruction will usually be disclosure of the spirits, such as men dressed in formidable *dukduk* (male-spirit) masks covering the whole body (among the Tolai), or the playing of sacred flutes, as voices of the ancestral spirits, in the house of 'the tabued man' (*mapil'yi*), who has dedicated himself in temporary priest-like fashion to his clan's prosperity and success in war (Wahgi). These indelible first impressions are intended to instil utter obedience to the instructors, one of whose primary aims is to impart the skills and strict regulations of fighting. This is why moments of physical ordeal and testing are crucial for achieving manhood, in the intended melding of cooperative clansman and uncowering warrior. A

Figure 3 Ilaga Dani boys, women and old men in support of warriors near the fight-ground, Highlands, West Papua. Photo: gift of R. Mitton.

lesser trial found in Wahgi practice has elders, especially maternal uncles, pushing boys closer and closer to a fire to withstand both fear and dehydration (Trompf 2008a: 90). An equivalent at Ilahita Arapesh initiations was the mock but scary armed 'attack' on novices by initiators (Tuzin 1980: 62–63); and more extreme methods in other Sepik contexts can entail serious scarification (thousands of small cuts for a crocodilian effect, for Sawos youths), the penis being temporarily sliced open longwise and bound back with healing leaves (Negrie-Yangoru), or even the requirement of initiands to show involvement in a first kill, following junior participation in a raiding party (Iatmül) (Gesch 2001: 1, 5–6, 10; Bateson 1958: 6–7; Trompf 2008a: 26–27, 90–91).

To illustrate the integral relationship between religion and violence in the initiatory rites of youths, consider the *mumingtain* ceremony among the Mumeng (Morobe highlands, New Guinea), when young men come out of their separation and display their acquired strength in all its glory within the context of the two main kinds of exchange ceremonies between allied tribes. The insignia of this strength, indeed of alleged invulnerability, is a shiny red mixture called *wawe*. Two substances are necessary for its composition. First was the special fat from inside of pigs' stomachs (called *memo*), prohibited to women and farmed only from beasts killed in the relevant ceremonies called *Sawump* and *Do*. When enacting these events, the rites and dances invoke Nendo, the primal ancestral figure behind each family-line (*gangun*), the Mumeng having possessed no generic name for ancestors but only a lineage's listed attestation of connection to Nendo's firstborn, Bambiek. The fertility that assures every *gangun*'s continuity together, and indeed general fecundity (of plants, pigs etc.), lies in the persistence of Nendo's seed (expressed as *memo-mame*, his greased penis). *Memo* grease (*sip*) was stored in bamboo tubes and stacked in the rafters of the male cult house (*umukmau*), with the greatest precaution to prevent spillage. The second substance was the red pandanus fruit (*marita*), available especially through trade with the Watut tribes to the south (and commonly eaten as a sweet). *Memo* and *marita* were brought into contact with each other at initiations, and permission has been granted to provide a public explanation of it here for the first time.

After their time of seclusion and training, the novices (eleven to fifteen years of age) are lined up standing and given a summary of key behavioural instructions – do not eat with strangers, do not steal women, marry when your beard has grown and so on – and then painted in stripes over the torso and limbs with what their paternal uncles had prepared, the shiny red grease called both *sip* (as marking a youth's particular lineage) and *wawe* (which expresses achieved initiation as male warrior). Anyone whose hands or feet touches *wawe* courts sickness, possibly death. It is carefully painted on, using sticks, and the initiates must let the substance dry by sitting up all night. In the morning the boys leave seclusion for the last time and present themselves publicly, even before women and children. But this display is the very time when 'religion' and 'the requirements of violence' dissolve in an indelible nexus: to the singing of their sponsors and elders, they stand joined in a line and sway in a 'roughly prepared' dance like a coloured serpent, to be 'taken' by *wawe*, as the power of Nendo's invulnerability. Indications of possession can be detected when some of the novices vomit, but a healer (*welo/welau*) is on hand with a special frog, who will expect to hear a confession that explains the faltering. At the rite's end, the newly initiated all line up and individually shout, so that the Ancestral Spirit is released out of each. It only remains for the *wawe* to be carefully removed in seclusion, and then the boys have the right to enter the male cult house and participate in fighting.[19]

We are not to forget initiation belonging to females, usually more quietly drawn out and especially focused on marriage, birthing and child-rearing, but hardly without attention to group loyalty. Male initiatory processes, moreover, do not stop at mere access to adult male company. There are new experiences to be had in cultic lore, hunting, protecting domesticated pigs, courtship and marriage, and important involvement in ceremonial exchange and battle. Learning types of hunting mentally connects to the way different martial strategies and situations are distinguished, while learning to 'read' flora and fauna builds confidence and heightened authority (Bulmer 1968). In some societies (one thinks of the Baktaman, upper Sepik), various grades of initiation into environal knowledge, specialization and shared ritual secrets apply (Barth 1975; cf. Allen 1967 more broadly). Or the time comes, as in the Ilahita Arapesh case, when men who become recognized cultic artists gain access to the 'towering' multitude of awesome creations in the darkness of the dreaded Nggwal's *tambaran* house (Tuzin 1980: 238).

Here perhaps we should raise the vexed question of sexual 'violation'. A small minority of cultures expected ritual homosexual acts on recently or partly initiated youths from older males (whether anally, by mouth or sperm anointing), for reasons usually related to group survival. In the well-known Marind-Anim instance (from the southern hinterland of West Papua), such practices would 'rebirth' young males away from their mothers, preparing them to contribute to vigorous headhunting raids (Van Baal 1966: 143–167, 671, 954). To cite Papua New Guinea highland cases, these acts meant passing down the 'vital essence' for future group

---

[19] My main informants were (permission-giver) Bundum Kwanatumb and Martin Tapei (May–June 1983), both of the Samburia lineage, as father and son covering two generations of *wawe* initiation.

strength (because boys are not taken to be born with semen in them, as the Sambia held) (Herdt 1993: 167–210); or by ingesting semen by fellatio from older youths as celestial-ancestral 'bone power', a young boy (even a six-year old) can create a young 'bodily ossuary' for his father (Iqwaye-Yagwoia) (Mimica 2007: 85–86, 92). And some occasions could demand 'disturbing' incidents of ritual sexual intercourse. In a rare great ceremony for the Mewun (southwest Malekula, Vanuatu), women from related districts were necessarily chosen, lined up lying down clothed by mats in the cult house of the great culture hero's wife, and penetrated by clan magicians in turn, basically to ensure general fertility but also, despite often incurring incest, to clinch the magicians' semi-priestly high-initiatory status (Deacon 1934: 651–654). Questions of cultural sensitivity and ethical evaluation vis-à-vis such violation-looking phenomena will produce endless debate, but one should not balk at including them in this study.

### 2.2.1.3 *On the Rationale of War and Its Sequential Acts*

It is time to consider indigenous warring itself and other belligerent acts of violence between enemy parties. In my volume *Payback* (Trompf 2008a) I have already written enough about the causation and reasons for group conflict in the 'black islands', and here I will only summarize my position. While admitting that surrounding circumstances can seriously affect people's behaviour, I put the onus of tribal fighting on human purposes and seriously question that factors external to human decision should be made central (as against subsidiary) in explaining it. Best known among such posited exterior factors are the effects of eco-systemic cycles and changes (especially the relative availability of land and food to handle population pressures), as in the older analyses of Andrew Vayda (1976: 9–42), who founded the journal *Human Ecology*; and the general-psychological theory that human groups simply have to let off steam, preferably in an outward direction, to benefit their stability, as an early theorist of Melanesian warfare, Camilla Wedgwood, averred, remarkably within the opening major article of the journal *Oceania* (1930). In response, my own views are not out of kilter with Karl Marx's insight that people 'make their own history', even if under prior 'circumstances' not 'chosen by themselves' ([1852] 1951: 225); but my stand is more in concert with Robin

Collingwood's grasp of human intents as 'purposive causation' (1939: 285–288), and so, whether they be well grounded or not, indigenous repertories of reason for engaging in conflict (and the local rationalities they reflect) should be our major explanatory port of call (Trompf 2008a: 37–41). On my reading of the very many different contexts in which I have undertaken fieldwork (from the West Papua Dani to the occupants of Bau islet, Fiji), I assess the fundamental rationale for traditional fighting to be an intergroup history of blood revenge, with secondary causes or 'triggers' for individual conflicts being aggravating instances of homicide, rape, abduction, serious 'insult', theft, attempts to take over land or other resources (salt, fresh water, fish etc.), serious failure to fulfil obligations, impatience in ceremonial contexts when the hosts are too late to deliver their gifts, and so on. Personal and kin-related pressure to make up for the loss of life eruptively taken from a security circle or solidary unit ('as if a hand were wrenched from the body', in Siassi [New Guinea] Islands metaphor) has been the key impetus to mobilize for violent action, and reactions to news and evidence of single severe acts of hostility are almost always read within this wider context of common-enough conflict. The arguments or logic applied are ubiquitously those of paying back negatively, of feeling being 'moved in the belly' to assuage the spilt blood and in a basic sense falling 'suddenly guilty' of insufficient action until appropriate retaliation is made (*pring pangwo!* in New Guinea highlander Chimbu utterance). Such pressure is born most intensely by the most affected families, or those who 'own' a particular quarrel within the revenge syndromes of ongoing intertribal troubles, and patterns of relationship will determine who will be readiest to support the aggrieved core. External allies, first to be called upon if needs be, will be warriors connected through marriage to those suddenly forced into mourning. Connected clan leaders, especially with rhetorical skills and a good memory of incidents and clashes, are likely to be called upon to stir and persuade.[20]

---

[20] The various issues and feelings documented are discussed in Trompf (2008a: 27–41). In work unfamiliar with my own, Jared Diamond (2013: 125, 157–159) adds to revenge as a primary cause the belief that the enemy are 'not human' (put as the words of a Wililiman Dani warrior, West Papuan highlands), yet with the

Concerning the actions surrounding war, it simply behoves us here to clarify that connections between 'religious activity' and 'mobilized violence' are everywhere. War as 'secular', or even as 'basically a game', does not apply, even if discerning 'the religious' takes the field-researcher's time. To fill out my position, here I take my cue from the son of an elderly Nali tribal warrior, Michael Sapau, from inland Manus (Usiai or Wisiai, northern New Guinea Islands, a culture distinct from the south coast one studied by Margaret Mead). In reflecting on his own father's warrior days, he distinguishes long-term preparations; immediate preparations; the day(s) of actual fighting; and a fight's immediate aftermath (Sapau and Tapo in Trompf 2008b: 38–40).

*Long-term preparations* may be distinguished in their spiritual and material expressions. Revenge syndromes are rarely so matter of fact as one might imagine in Melanesia, as if it were just a matter of tallying losses in the field of open physical conflict. Any death could be suspicious: very many of them (all, in some cultures) would be put down to sorcery, mostly that of outside enemies and not necessarily on a battlefield. When a death occurred by sickness, many cultures had their distinct divining procedures to discover the spiritual source of the fatality. Mendi mourners (Papua New Guinea [PNG] Southern Highlands), for example, poked a hollowed bamboo stick into the grave at night to seek indications from the interred victim. The aggrieved kin can also choose to sleep together, linked by cordyline rope near the burial, and supervised by a 'dream interpreter' who would wake and query visible stirrers as to any culprit suggested in their dreams (Lornley 1976). More spectacularly, the Bena Bena (PNG Eastern Highlands) will expect a near relative of someone recently dying from sickness to be temporarily possessed by the deceased and then to run full pelt as a 'payback runner', even winding across rough terrain, to pinpoint a track leading to the guilty party's hamlet (Trompf 2008a: 33–35). Such

common absence of generic words for 'human', the case needs to be carefully made (given that words conveying 'stranger' and 'fearful other' are always present). For precious detailing of the role persuasive rhetoric has in central New Guinea highland intertribal relations, see Merlan and Rumsey (1991: 109–11 et passim) (central New Guinea highland Temboka).

divining, dreams being interpreted as well (cf. Stephen 1980: 27–31), usually does not result in immediate action: warriors will bide their time, discussing an appropriate occasion for action, perhaps sending an armed party to make the accusation (often by oracular shouting in the located hamlet's 'piazza' or 'dance-ground', in case the accused group may rebuff the imputations convincingly) or testing their own alternative views to avoid breaking a useful alliance. Besides, if tracing matters precisely is too hard, going for a more vulnerable (yet suitable) enemy target may satisfy for the time being. Numerous background undercurrents, then, may need to be probed by researchers as ongoing wars work themselves out.

Before any outbreak of hostilities, warrior novices have to be instructed as to their subsidiary roles, connections with allies have to be consolidated and weapons have to be prepared – some, like pineapple-shaped stone war clubs among the Fuyughe, taking months to carve, and most etched with some protective insignia or bespelled by the war magician or supportive sorcerer (Trompf 2004: 27 and pl. [8]; cf. Hiltbrand 1962: 27, pl. 13). When raids on water were to be undertaken, new war canoes might have to be patiently hollowed by stone adzes, while being designed and fitted out with the magical aid of religious specialists. The Roviana, eerily, before their seagoing head-hunting expeditions to Bougainville, would use the bodies of recently killed captives as rollers to launch a large vessel (*tomoko*), with the corpses then being ritually cannibalized to mark the crucial occasion (Wright 2013: 19–58). Over war matters one finds consultations and conversations constantly burbling under the surface of daily life. Among the Wahgi, each tribe will have in their clans at least one or two 'tabued men', as mentioned before, strictly confined with their wives to a fenced-off area and cult-house even for up to twenty years, always seeking to communicate with 'the spirits of the fighting dead' between great pig feasts and continually calculating which tribe deserves vengeance and which concessions. Clan leaders ('big men') and senior warriors, in their daily debates about the course of things, dare not neglect paying heed to these *mapil'yi*s' adjudgements for decision-making with allies if a clash is impending and deserves involvement (Swain and Trompf 1995: 142–143). In highland cases, where large numbers of people are mobilized for war on different ridges above fight-grounds, negotiations can be incessantly in 'process' (as famously among the New Guinea highland Maring), decisions being affected by whether tribal collusions have altered in balance, key figures have been killed, climate conditions for plant growth and harvesting are satisfactory, and occasions for ceremonial exchange, marriages, alliances and pork consumption have been pulled off (Foin and Davis 1984).

*Shorter-term preparations* ubiquitously included the prohibition against sexual relations the night before an expected fight: the loss of semen incurred loss of vitality ('life' with religious connotations).[21] The warriors would normally be in each other's company, in the male cult- or club-house, except for night-watchers and spies scouting in enemy territory. Sapau writes of the Usiai that the night before participants went out from the 'men's round house', they were tested by 'the war magician … for any bad omens', and if any had a violent physical reaction to the sniffing of his lime-gourd they were advised to stay back for the day. He would offer a ginger and herbal mixture (a later part of the initiation process if novices were involved), and his was the task to check and magically protect the warriors' chosen path, while before starting out the clan leader invoked for group strength 'the spirits of the past mighty warriors' (in Trompf 2008b: 39).

Among the Wahgi, any bout of war would be opened with the killing of a larger pig, and the ordinary magician (*kunj°yi*) bespells into it *omblum* (life-energy), a central concept of their religious life. The war magician (*obokunjeyi*) had to concern himself with a number of issues before a field exchange. On an assumed understanding with his opposite number, he would mark an invisible line between selected bushes as marking the boundary warriors should not pass when letting loose their arrows or spears. At the fight itself, he would squat safely behind a stone and whistle – like a football umpire! – if his prescribed limits were foolishly crossed, signalling that a warrior had thereby lost the invulnerability given him before battle. Any fighter preparing himself could expect from magicians bespelled war-paint and the approval of headdresses, with a good knowledge of who was wearing which array of feathers (as distinguishable markers of the participants) and whether any feathers had been exchanged,

---

[21] On cosmic presuppositions surrounding bodily fluids and their loss, start with Stewart et al. (2001).

'borrowed' or even wrongly appropriated from their special storehouse (*mingar*).[22] For the Wahgi, sharing dreams has a crucial place for a warrior cohort: only waking dreams count, and sometimes a warrior is awoken if he shows restlessness at dawn, for oneiric contents can engender greater confidence or cautiousness (Trompf 2004: 110–122 [with other cases]).

It is folly to miss grasping *actual fighting* as a religious datum: the collaboration and back-up against the forces of death; the battle cries and the shrill whooping to mimic spirits; the taunting imprecations towards the foe; the sheer agility to avoid spears and arrows; and the heroism of those skilful enough to cause the enemy harm or sacrificial enough to retrieve a fellow's ailing body. In headhunting raids by the Elema (Papuan Gulf), it was a moment of sheer exhilaration to bring down the frame of a man-catcher (like a giant butterfly net; see Figure 4) over a fleeing victim, as the high point of both war and the hunt (Chalmers and Gill 1885 [opp. titl.]; Murray 1912: 145–146). There had to be a strange sense of humour imagining what cannibal enemy raiders did to your kin if they were caught, '"cutting you up and stuffing you into a string bag, taking you home and cutting you up more and cooking you with sago and greens' (as the Samo said of the Bedamini on the Strickland Plain, Papua, knowing they were capable of doing the same) (Shaw 1996: 24).

At the day's end or the onset of rain (which could damage precious feathers!), any success or disaster, typically small in field skirmishing with relatively inaccurate weaponry, would soon issue in impressive *post-action behaviour*. Drumming and dancing into the night would rub victory in for the adversaries; and for some groups (as with the Bena), securing a dead enemy meant acquiring immense strength from an immediate cannibal feast (Trompf 2008a: 52), while in others both one's own dead and killed enemies were consumed, women quickly cutting up body parts with baskets (Kunié, Isle of Pines, New Caledonia) (Ta'unga [1846] 1968: 86–91). Victory was an occasion not only for group-sustaining singing but also for recounting legends and exploits, even of women who killed men. Conversations to be had or songs made up following an intense confrontation were

[22] Trompf, Fieldnotes, 1975, 1980 (fight zones); cf. O'Hanlon, 1989: 23–38, and esp. 68 (post-pacification).

Figure 4 Etched image of an Elema man-catcher, Papuan Gulf (*ca.* 1879). Source: J. Chalmers and W. Gill, *Work and Adventures in New Guinea*, 1885, front.

potentially of 'epic proportions'. Even after three years, a Maisin warrior (Collingwood Bay, northern Papua) could recount every key detail of a revenge raid on the Are (Cape Vogel), the manoeuvres and the instruments used: Maisin 'poling sticks' to land their canoes, Are 'conch shells' sounding the alarm, the Maisin beheading an Are with 'a broad-bladed spear', with exchanges across the beach, in the trees, close to an Are palisaded village, in long treacherous grass, with one side or the other surging in (counter-) attack and taking an enemy, until the Maisin took to the water again, the whole story combining inspiration and lessons (Nortris or Nogar [?] in Stone-Wigg 1909: 16–20).

In contrast, women's ululations or wailing would mark a warrior's demise and preparations for funeral rites, with close kin often self-harming (perhaps cutting off a finger, pulling out their hair or starting to destroy the deceased's properties). Healers were typically on hand, most commonly females, attending to the wounded, their repertories always including 'prayer-utterances' and 'magical actions'. If a raiding party burnt a hamlet (as the author witnessed among the Fuyughe), better-defended friends and allies would have to take in refugees or decide on adoptions if parents were caught and children survived. And clan leaders had to think urgently about processes of compensation if a man from an allied tribe was hit (for inadequate negotiations could bring on worrisome discord with traditional supporters), usually a victim's mother and her brother (the maternal uncle) being promised gifts. Among the Usiai, the first moves to honour the dead were signalled by a sombre beating of a large trunk-hewn slit-gong (*gar-amut*), and a few pigs were sought to be slaughtered to mark and make up for his going to the ancestors. As for any enemy carcasses procured, they were traded to the cannibal Lou islanders (in the Rambutyo group south of Manus) for black obsidian blades best serving to cut and kill (Sapau in Trompf 2008b: 34–35, 39–40). On the opposite, southern side of the great New Guinea island, the headhunting Western Elema, expectedly, were bent on keeping heads as trophies, but, with the skulls arranged on racks beside each clan-emblem boards (*gopi*), they also served as compensatory mementos of past warriors within the darkness of the towering cathedral-like men's house (*eravo*) (Trompf 2004: pl.[6]).

Sufficient triumph could allow the victor to try imposing peace: the 'Ned Kelly' of Melanesian warfare, the Western Mekeo chief Ikaroa Raepa, unbeatable behind his thick bark armour, magnanimously achieved long-lasting quiet relations with the neighbouring far-Eastern Elema at a volatile culturo-linguistic boundary (*estim. ca.* 1780) (Trompf 1977; Avosa [forthcoming]), In a comparable highland context, Wahgi Kumai tribesmen could stave off trouble with their next-door Chimbu contestants (the Endugla tribe) by signalling their willingness for peace, the war-magician making a ritual meal of the hardest and driest variety of banana to express disdain for military inaction. Participants know full well the procedures mean nothing if the Endugla were not doing likewise at the same time, and just in case, before they put their weapons in the rafters of the men's house, they put on a mock battle-front (see Figure 5) towards enemy lines (Trompf 2008b: 98).

Figure 5 Wahgi warriors in a last expression of aggression before storing weapons, New Guinea highlands. *Photo: by the author.*

Lineages in mourning for a loss would not fail to let the world know of their urge to avenge: south Wahgi tribes will mount avengeable corpses ostentatiously on a platform, whereas warriors thought to die fittingly were immediately buried away (Ramsay 1975: 348). Motuan widows were expected to lie beside the corpses of their slain husbands for hours, whispering in their ears and, as days went on, smearing themselves with decaying flesh. Favouring big family houses, some on high stilts partly over quiet seawater, the Motu would even bury their dead in shallow, caged graves right under the floor, not just to honour them but to be close enough to divine from them who any unknown killers were, with whiffs of putrefaction reminding them to work for reprisal (Trompf 2008a: 306–307).

As a caveat here, while so much confirms the obvious significance of religion in upholding the place of war in Melanesian societies, please realize that so many components mentioned, outside fighting as such, are not in themselves violent, unless imposed by fierce-enough coercion. Mind you, before, during and mainly in the aftermath of major intergroup conflict anywhere in the Melanesian region, there were also leaders' judgements to be made about anybody who had 'gone against the rules', and we must now turn to the issue of punition.

### 2.2.1.4  *Violence in Sanction and Redress*

Patterns of violence in traditional Melanesian religions were hardly confined to the arena of war. We have to account for violent actions as *punishments* and also consider attempts to contain grievances within security circles. Of course, sanctions were imposed if accepted rules of engagement or commands by war leaders were broken. Using a pronged spear to upturn an enemy canoe in a Sepik River skirmish, for instance, or ambushing a village in which drums were being beaten were considered capital offences for the Iatmül. Across the board, those warriors taking impetuous or maverick action in field-war or raids could be dealt with severely. Citing Leopold Pospisil's famous work on legal anthropology, about the lower highland Kapauka (West Papua), young hotheads who disregarded military directions received a head-beating with a log, though a worse fate was reckoned to be the public and non-violent shaming for unwillingness to fight without worthy excuse (Pospisil 1958: 236–238). What we are now introducing are primarily the bodily consequences of committing delicts or offences. Only a careful feel into each culture will reveal the balance between what learned outside interpreters would call law and initiatory precepts (commonly in tok pisin [neo-Melanesian creol] as *lo*), regulation, time-honoured tradition (*pasin bilong tumbuna*), custom (*kastom*) and sacred prohibitions (*tambu*). Through the overlapping presence of all these, in Melanesian societies adolescents soon imbibe a moral regimen or a ready recognition of what is right and wrong for them in group life (with a prospect of earning respect through acceptable behaviour that, in time, induces leadership initiatives they would dare not show early in life).[23]

---

[23] To debate about imbibed morality and universal moral realism and deep-structured conscience independently of these considerations would be to misplace 'the mental dictionary' of things (to use Vichian language), because such abstractions as morality (rather than good or bad deeds), truth (as against 'telling it true' or

What is wrong demands paying back (negatively), and the word(s) for this punishing are most often the same as for taking revenge, because wrongdoing, as an assault against one's own safety net and the particular people in it, creates a debt as liability (e.g., Wahgi: *kumap*), just as inter-tribal killing does, and is distinct from an act of positive exchange or gift-giving (Wahgi: *pundum*), even though the latter also implies the pressure of reciprocal payback. Sometimes even the one word, such as *kukgi* used by the upper Ok Tedi River Faiwolmin (highland PNG Western Province) can denote a generic 'paying-back' – that is, for 'revenge (in warfare, through sorcery, etc.), ... fulfilling obligations in trade, ceremonial exchange, etc.)' and 'punishment (for the breaking of a tabu, disobeying fight leaders' orders, etc.)' (Trompf 2000: 61). We are not to forget the relativities of punition, of course. As rules of thumb, the isolated killing of a stranger or raping of a woman from among the enemy after a chance encounter would be tolerated, but if the victim turned out to be related to an ally, the deed could be disastrous and thus punishable. In exogamous societies, if a man commits adultery the death penalty is less likely than for a woman, because she would have thereby shown disloyalty as an outsider within a solidary group meant to stay close-knit (Trompf 2008a: 84). Husbands would be ill advised to execute their adulterous wives without family or elder support: on Wogeo (off New Guinea's coast), a headman may claim this right, but for ordinary men it would be the equivalent of murder (Hogbin 1978: 116). Where execution was normal and expected, only social power might make a difference, as on Florida and Savo (central Solomons), where a chief could take an accused highly ranked adulteress as his 'concubine' (*rembi*) (Codrington 1891: 243). Then again, some rules are shared as inviolable between in- and out-groups. In negotiating an alliance, anyone who chances to knock a Mekeo peace chief's ceremonial gourd (*fa'onga*) would be instantly despatched by warriors on both sides of a dispute, and one simply had to steel oneself to take the action (Trompf and Hau'ofa 1974: 234, 236).

lying) and so on barely show up linguistically. For the debates, involving R. Shweder and J. Robbins, see especially Cassanti (2014) and Hickman (2014); compare Barker (2007); Trompf (2008a: 16–17 et passim).

There were no gaols in traditional Melanesia. Punitive action was open. Captured enemy victims were tied up temporarily, usually with ritual slaying in view. If they were young they might be taken in, even married: in the southern Torres Strait Islands, mainland Aboriginal youths dubbed *gassimigi* ('caught ones') were intriguingly treated this way (Swain 1993: 82; cf. Trompf 2008a: 53, 84, 112). Under the matrilineal *susu* system of the Papuan Massim, powerful women could drop their grass skirt on a youngster to make a claim of adoption, while most captives would be tortured facing the recently bereaved; under such a female aegis, male adulterers were more likely to be killed (though 'the *susu* could be rent' if someone acted too hastily over a sexual outrage), whereas female culprits were thrashed or sent to a far-off though connected family (Seligman 1910: 555–556; Romilly 1887: 36; Fortune [1932] 1963: 61). Again, some delicts are left for the spirits to punish (such as taking fruit from trees tabued for the dead, as among the Wahgi) (Ramsay 1975: 154); some can be paid off by shell-money fines or vigorous destruction of one's property (among the Tolai policed by Tabuans, wearing the mask of the female-spirit who gave birth to the *Dukduk*s); and others again by open reprimanding, though the shame of these matters can feel like weapons on the body (Rickard 1891: 71; Epstein 1984).[24] The deployment of sorcery punitively, of course, comes into the equation, as well as actions against sorcerers and witches, but we shall have to put such matters into a wider picture later. In an intriguing transference of violence to the spirit-world, we learn of Wango River 'wizards' (on west San Cristoval, Solomons) being paid a pig to 'fight' or ward off or at least charm ghost-sprits (*ataro*), as a means of getting back at someone using them inimically, whether without or within the group (Codrington 1891: 196; Fox and Drew 1915: 133–135). And then there are unusual instances of 'violent requiting' against deceased individuals within the security circle: the quick burial and non-performance of normal funerary rites for unproductive (usually long-disabled) individuals (Waim [Dreikikir, East Sepik]), or a husband burying a fractious wife head-

---

[24] Compare Nida (1954: 130), seminal on honour-shame vis-à-vis guilt-innocence cultures. This is not to forget the psychological effects of elders' and leaders' curses; see, for instance, Crawley (1934: 5, 10, 19, 21, 24–28).

downward, to avert her return as a ghost if and when he takes another wife (Wahgi) (Trompf 1979: 129, 216 n. 26). The latter case reminds one that the Wahgi (especially the Kuma tribe documented by Marie Reay) believe in different expressions of witchcraft, one of which can involve a wife turning out to be too loyal to her birth-tribe in a time of tension. Certainly, when a 'big man' died, a party would be sent to consult enemy war-magicians as to whether such a woman might have smuggled in items prepared by outside sorcerers. The punishment, however, was banishment, a relief to a clan made nervous by multiple witchcraft accusations (Reay 1987: 98–100).

Some of these last cases bring us to the issue of violence and personal redress. Individuals (usually agnates) belonging to an in-group (or persons connected affinally) can fall out badly. This often occurs through verbal insult or a taunting act (such as deliberately eating someone else's totem in front of them). The reaction is not usually individualist: the aggrieved party will enlist his lineage or clan members for support in a group ('gang-like') reprisal, traditionally not involving formal weaponry but wooden staves, offenders and offended settling with bruising or excited buffeting. Inter-lineage conflict can be settled by a ritual confronting (Trompf 2008a: 91–93). In the Kuma (south Wahgi) fashion, men will stand in line opposite each other and kick shins (a 'game' called *tagba boʒ*) until one side withdraws (Reay 1974: 203). Personal redress is rare, as between warrior rivals in a 'face-off' (over women or in competitive jibes), but when, in such a cognatic society as the Huli, a crowd gathered to witness them, serious violence was avoided, the opponents shouting formulaic imprecations at each other in a chosen public space, slapping each other's faces with pieces of pork, and declaring their own ears would stop hearing or their penises would fall off if their claims were not true (Glasse 1965: 40).

A special combination of physical punishment and redress can hardly be overlooked: domestic violence. Of course, we cannot expect traditional life-ways to keep uniform standards on the custodianship of women and children, and I distil matters only from depth of experience and wide reading. Generally, women do not fare as well as men, because in most societies they are 'acquired' through bride-payments as special 'possessions' (by a lineage supporting the groom, and more for congealing intergroup bonds than 'out of love'). Where women in rare cases could enjoy adelphic polyandrous relations, or (as with the Massim) a stronger physical bearing, they were in a good position to circumvent male violence (e.g., Rivers 1914: 127). The same applied when male and female ceremonial activity, sung myths and ritual theater were taken as 'antiphonally necessary' for group life, as among the New Guinea Eastern highlander Gimi, whose myth about the first marriage (resulting in the wife murdering the husband) demands the constant repairing of order between the sexes (Gillison 1993: 65–153, esp. 97). In coastal and island Austronesian contexts, we see Trobriand women dominating certain rites, their assertive coming-and-going across the village arena in the mortuary exchange or *sagali* ceremonies of banana leaf (*tagini*) being a striking example (Weiner 1983: 73–76). And in villages where family household dwellings prevailed (the Motu), bride prices could be generously high for a woman both prized and cherished (Parratt 1971).[25]

Women, expectedly, have their own accepted 'theaters' of violence, especially in parenting or with older women chastising younger ones in families. In the ritual contexts of the women's cult, physical discipline by supervisors is hardly unknown (cf. Kyakas and Weissner 1992). Moreover, in a Wahgi courting ritual in which I was participant observer, set in a longhouse for guests from other clans and tribes, a strong and reputably disciplinarian old woman sat at one end as stern regulator: watching the long lines of youths and maidens as they sat opposite and brushed their head-hair lightly against each other, she was ready to beat any young man smartly on the shoulder with a thick wooden club if he ventured too far. Otherwise any perceived lack of obedience on females' parts, or disloyalty to the husband's family, tabu-breakage, neglect in garden work, child- or pig-rearing, and any change in bodily appearance (very often slackened breasts) or allegedly strange behaviour (suggesting witchcraft) can place a woman in jeopardy of masculine pushes and fists, causing injury or worse. The non-culpability for an Asaro husband to thrust a stick into his wife's vagina, just out of suspicion of sexual waywardness, rates as perhaps the worst scenario (Read 1966: 213; Trompf 2008a: 86–89).

---

[25] For the Trobriands I also rely on my own field documentation (September 2012); and for the Motu on work with S. Kopi (1996).

Occasionally women's self-harm could be expected, suicide apparently more frequent among young females, over unrequited love, after public shaming, revenge on oppressive husbands or group maltreatment (Stewart and Strathern 2003; Trompf 2008a: 88). At the loss of their male keepers, in extreme cases widows offered their lives. Lemakot childless widows (New Ireland) were expected to be strangled and then thrown, suttee-like, on their husband's funeral pyres (Bodrogi 1967: 71–72), while among the nearby Barok a choice could be made for a human sacrifice between the wife and the deceased man's child (Jessep 1974: 203–14; cf. Lockerby [1809] 1925 on Fijian widow strangling). Most commonly in funerary contexts elsewhere, mourners of both sexes will self-harm less drastically or express sorrow through wounding a child. And the transference of 'temperamental relativities' to the handling of children has been a matter of prolonged scholarly discussion. In the Sepik, whereas Arapesh groups are very indulgent with infants, Chambri Lakes children are threatened against crying; the highland Gimi resolutely smack young miscreants, as typical for the region – indeed, among the far western Wahgi, parents would tie a thieving child up to a tree for the night as punishment (Mead 1950: 49–51; 154; Gillison 1993: 95; Parake 1983: 4). Off the Papuan coast, I recorded, a Roro father promptly dunks a small child into the brine from a canoe for grizzling in stormy or becalming weather; while Papua Highland Koiari women often literally scratched their irritating offspring with the kind of severity that reflected a high level of intergroup tension. Such data can only serve as relevant pointers in a study of violence, not to depreciate a wealth of cultures that have nurtured relationships in survivalist mode.

It would be remiss to pass over custodianship of the (non-infantine) vulnerable. Literature is pretty threadbare on this subject, but violent frustration in the care of the sick, elderly and dying in Melanesia is hard to find, though relative neglect of them for not knowing how to cope is common enough (Strathern 1968; Gibbs 2003). What happens, though, when individuals difficult to accommodate in their abnormal behaviour turn violent? Again, case studies are limited, but some are very interesting, especially from the highlander Maring, with the phenomenon of 'temporary madness as theater'. That is, any dangerously deranged individual, possibly armed, will create a highly dramatic scene that draws community onlookers.

The 'wild one' is followed around, often with loud hubbub and hilarity, yet watched carefully, with chasers scattering when threatening behaviour suddenly erupts, perhaps with the swinging of an axe, and all serves as farce and entertaining spectacle until the victim of the 'attack', often reckoned possessed, subsides back into a 'normalcy' (Clarke 1973 [on the Maring]; cf. Newman 1964 [Asaro]; Young 1971: 133–137 [Massim "amok"]; with Burton-Bradley 1976: 50–62).

### 2.2.1.5  *Violence against Animals, and Sacrifices*

Nothing but thorough study can intimate the associations when one serious event produces violent responses internal to a group, as when a great man dies and mourning relatives may cut off their child's finger (Mae Enga), or the man's property will be destroyed in a kind of cleansing anger (as with Tolai). In certain times of the year, even certain abrupt actions in gardening can evoke associations of killing; Sangara Orokaiva men sever the heads of their harvested taro as if each is a human victim, and with a classified name. Their children will learn that if they are caught by the enemy, early or late in life, they will divulge their name before dying, because the killer, asking for it, will name his own (future) child after it, as a combination of power and compensation (Schwimmer 1973: 111–137; compare Figure 6). Aside from other questions about violence against inert objects, some attention clearly needs to be paid to the despatching of animals, especially, since this is an Element about religion, in cultic contexts.

Melanesia holds high interest for its varieties of sacrificial procedures, including the use of elaborate altar arrangements (as among the Solomonese Toambaita, north Malaita). The PNG highland region is famous for the mass slaughtering of pigs, which cannot be passed off as 'animal-killing festivals' when on close inspection they are typically acted out to please the ancestors. As a general rule, 'you cannot eat your own pigs' after such slaughter (Rubel and Rosman 1978); the hosts who have brought the beasts together in a ritual context must give generously to the affinal relatives and allies who are invited, precisely because the dead will feel their prior work for group security has been reaffirmed. The visitors (including those coming to negotiate marriages, with even formerly

DAKODAKO, THE MAN EATER.

Figure 6 Wedau warrior stands over his young victim, Papuan north coast. *Photo: staged by P.J. Money for A. Ker,* Papuan Fairy Tales, 1910.

estranged parties being wooed as potential allies) will be 'wounded' enough to ask whether their own clan could put on as spectacular and generous an event in their turn. Here we are just reminding readers that, after the days of dancing or display are over, serious violence can (re)occur (Feil 1987: 39–61, 233–70).[26]

As one who has witnessed over 200 pigs felled in four hours by clubbing at the strong hands of clansmen of the Senglep tribe at Bolba (Wahgi), I am bound to admit that, through all the squealing and odd cases of the mis-hitting with thick wooden staves, it was a brutal spectacle. Butchering was in the open air for all to see if they wished, and men, women and children soon knew where to line up to receive the meat portions due to them. Significantly, many pig jaws were kept as prizes, to be dried and hung up in different edifices or on marker-posts as trophies, as if commemorating victory (Trompf 2007: 146–149). While in the Wahgi case personal prestige from group and ancestral acceptance come with acquiring pigs to give away, elsewhere, as on Little Malo (off Espiritu Santo, Vanuatu), more and more awesome power resided in a chief from the mounting number of pigs he killed for the ancestors, by accruing their soul-power (Déniau 1901: 347). In some other contexts, fighting can break out in the context of pig-killing rituals. At a Fuyughe feast or *gab(e)*, put on in response to life-crisis transitions in a clan, after the preliminary sacrifice of dogs (see Figure 7), followed by days and nights of dancing, the custom is for the hosts to find the pigs for slaughter, but if they take too long the guests' patience can be frayed, since they themselves have had to work hard over months and offer preliminary gift-tokens (*seef*) to ensure their invitation, so an altercation can erupt, even a breakdown of alliance and consequent feuding if someone gets hurt in the dispute (Hirsch 2008: 24). In other cases, signals of cruelty to animals appear. To produce the fabled curled pig-tusks used for ceremonial, or worn to show higher initiatory or ritual grade status, as in the northern ni-Vanuatu islands, a young pig's upper canines are partially loosened (among with Sa [south Raga or Pentecost Is.] using a tapered pig jaw hammer), so that the lower canines grow 'unimpeded, in a circular fashion' (Huffman 2019: 203–204). The collective despatching of beasts by the Papuan highland Tauade was called a 'war on pigs', done ferociously to

---

[26] New Caledonia is sometimes placed as an exception to pig-killing festivals, yet compare Shineberg (1999: 3–10, 25–35), on young males competing through pig feasts.

Figure 7 A dog sacrifice preliminary to *Gab* festival and pig-kill, Fuyughe, Papuan highlands. *Photo: by the author.*

remind of the hosts' warrior power (Hallpike 1977: 74, 164–167). Selected butchers of the western Elema, who killed pigs for their guests during the *Hevehe* ritual in a more secluded space, used a dagger of cassowary bone or sharp stone to make a decisive thrust to an animal's heart, twisting and 'joggling the weapon … up and down, like a man pumping a tire'. One might miss the datum, too, that, following the Elema's whole festive spree, when mammoth *Hevehe* masks have been destroyed in the sea, parties among the jubilant and relieved hosts were not only ready to hunt for a bush-pig to feast upon themselves but also to seek a human victim, perhaps an enemy too inquisitive and thus too nearby, because only after such closing violence could all the celebrants' hornbill feathers be stowed away in the *eravo* (Williams [1940] 1977: 319–20, 375, 379–82, 385, 389).[27]

---

[27] Killing pigs by bow and arrow is a limited ritual practice; see, for example, Temple (2002: 126) (Airininip Dani).

This last datum raises the issue of sacrificing humans. This had a minority presence in Melanesia, although by now it might be hard to find memories of it. Fairly recently converted PNG Sepik highlander Oksapmin, though, confided that a sexually productive young man would be killed and severed (by specialists in a ritual named *Yuan hän*), his body parts shared among clans and buried in swampland to enhance local fertility (Brutti 1997: 90–100). Human sacrifice is more likely to show up in chiefly societies, as with the strangling of girls to accompany a dead Efate chief (Vanuatu) to the other side (Gill in Moss 1925: 202–203; cf. Section 1.2 on Roy Mata and Section 2.3.2.1 in this Element). It has been most notoriously associated with eastern Viti Levu and Bau islet, Fiji, where male victims replaced pigs (used ritually elsewhere in the island complex, even if with some human captives as well). From Bau, the highest (virtually 'royal') chief or *vunivalu* was lord over a peculiar network, 'raw women' being acquired in exchange for 'cooked men'. Bau and its close allies widened their power-sphere by pressuring other tribes to 'owe fealty', especially by offering marriageable females to warrior parties ('fisher-of-turtle' assassin tribesmen) who were willing to bring in sacrificial captives to Bau. These were the fierce ones, each committing himself 'to die at his point of rock' in the task (as the Fijian proverb still has it), the very opposite to the coward (*daturu*) who kept his club 'unstained with blood' and would forever pound excrement with it in the hell-like under-land of *Bulu*. Mostly enemies from along the Rewa coast, the victims were beheaded and then cut up at Bau (history's 'capital of cannibalism') (Sahlins 1983: 73–93; cf. Williams 1858: 215–233; Clunie 1977: 50; Thomson 2008: 352). Devouring the eyes and liver signified vanquishing the enemy's *mana* ('empowering'), and delicately carved forks (*iculanibokoloa*s) had to be employed to drop human flesh into the mouth, since the use of lips was tabued. To this day, visitors to the islet can see the arresting upright stone used for beheadings in the large Ratu Seru Cakobau Church, the stone's notch at the top now poignantly used as a baptismal font! Ironically, the *vunivalu* or 'root' of war, always selected from the prestigious Tui Kaba clan, was thought of as a cannibal victim himself at his own installation and a 'stranger' to the whole system he maintained, waiting (after his death emplaced within Melanesia's largest known tomb complex) to be reborn as a local deity or *kalou yalo*). Women were sent to him as wives (he had up to forty); in a large swimming pool on Bau they regularly consorted with him; and the multiplicity of his offspring serviced the trading of young females. In return, in stone-ringed arenas, at Bau but also elsewhere in the network, one role for a priest (*bete*) was to be ritual executioner, so enhancing his own pretensions to greatness within the chief-connected families. Priests or priestesses were key councillors in military operations, glorying in their gods' area of control as a 'small war club' (in the skiting phrase of an officiant of the high Snake God Ndengei), and they received a spear from each successful warrior after a killing to acknowledge their protective power (cf. Fison 1884; Hocart 1927: 1–11; Sokiveta 1973: 94–98; Toren 1995: 62–67; Dyson 1996: 77; Thomson 2008: 347). The building completion of edifices for rites and chiefly councils usually involved sacrificing a few captives throughout Melanesian Fiji, and to the north-east, at Somosomo, Taveula Island, arriving Methodist missionaries pleaded against 'sixteen women' being 'strangled in honour of the young chief' who had just died (in 1839) (Williams 1858: 222; Williams and Calvert 1884: 252–253; cf. Thomas 1997: 198).

## 2.1.1.6 Sorcery and Witchcraft

What about distinctly spiritual negativities? Do they also belong with phenomena of violence in Melanesia? This is an interesting question. When the Abelam (Sepik) spoke proverbially of sorcery as 'the spear by night', they meant that daylight fighting could be kept up nocturnally by enemy-directed spirit-power that was thus implicated in war (Forge 1970: 259). From specialists bespelling weapons to the accompanying of warriors into fight zones by 'workers of adverse magic', sorcery activity presents a distinctly religious component within the bodily onrushes of conflict between 'out-groups' (Patterson 1974: 132–160; 45, 3; 1975: 212–234), and the fear of witches, especially flying ones that are still reported to appear at night along the Papuan coasts and island chains, are usually mentally sourced back to traditional enemy groups (Fortune [1932] 1963: 7, 150, 152, 261, 295, 297). But of course a problem for our discussion is that sorcerers' and witches' work seems to elude and surpass physicality, and an observer sceptical about their effects might only want to set aside this aspect of things as imaginary. These difficulties acknowledged, though, we still have to include highly relevant data, because so-called 'assault sorcery' comes into the picture, and in the self-stated repertory of techniques of spirit-workers themselves, a distinction will often seem drawn between 'non-empirical magic manoeuvres' and plainly physical procedures.

Assault sorcery was first reported for coastal and island Papua at least from 1908 and commonly goes by the name *vada*: two or more sorcerers surprise someone in the bush, virtually killing them yet administering a poison to cause a dazed recovery, before death follows. Although 'the wholeness of the body' can be 'inspected' after the incident, and victims can sometimes recount what happens to them as horrific, it is difficult to agree with Reo Fortune that this just 'remains sorcery, not violence' or is basically the result of 'hypnotism' (Fortune [1932] 1963: 184–187, esp. 187). And it is even harder to take this line in the cases of so-named *sanguma* (Sepik River cultures), when victims allege that, surprised, surrounded and stunned, they have watched such objects as stones being placed into their bodies and sewn up and then been left to wander around utterly ill. I interviewed one such victim who learnt of my presence at the Yangoru Catholic Mission (hinterland East Sepik) in 1981: he spoke of being violently bashed by younger men and fed on a yellow liquid, which an older healer, knowing the typical use of pulped centipede in *sanguma*, fortunately got him to vomit up (Oral test [=OT] O. Lanaro; cf. Gesch 2015; Gibbs and Wailoni 2009). *Vele* 'death sorcery' on the Solomon Islands (from Lauman, Russell Islands, north-west off Guadalcanal) looks comparable: the practitioner mesmerizes his human prey by swinging a special string bag (*vele*) of poisoned mangos, then tipping portions of them into the mouth and injecting stingray spines under the finger- and toenails. The victim is jolted awake, and a disgusting stench indicates to the (quickly hiding) sorcerer that his efforts have worked: yet the victim senses nothing is awry, goes about his business and suddenly collapses a few hours after (Hogbin 1964: 56–57).

Whether a conceptual distinction is clearly registered by practitioners or not, in the most widespread pattern of sorcery action the sorcerer's repertory can involve spells and heating rituals at a distance (on an intended victim's hair, fingernails or other acquired 'leavings' in a small net bag, with the specialist's stones and shells kept under sweat of his armpit) *and yet* can also include the plain act of doing violence by poisoning or secreting a venomous snake near a sleeper's room-space.[28] Whether real or imagined, harm from an animal can also be put down to sorcery, and in the Fuyughe mindset just being brushed by a runaway cassowary thought to be ridden by a sorcerer can be enough to bring on a deadly tropical ulcer psychosomatically (Fastré 1937: 187–188; cf. Bartle 2005: 224–225 on the Kobon). Allegedly violent actions call for consideration here: such spirit-workers' operations defy empirical investigation, but they are typically held capable of manipulating dangerous material objects – a Gelaria witch (South Massim), for example, is said to translocate as a shadow, project sharp slivers of coral or human tooth or bone into her victim to cause a full-body rash, and then escape as a snake that returns to her anus (Seligman 1910: 640–641).

We shall soon have to come back to questions of changes in the position of sorcery and witchcraft after outside pressures to stop tribal warfare incurred important side effects; but in any case, ahead of such pacification, those with the power of working inimical magic, and thus sorcerers alongside war magicians, were accepted as very useful for group security. And when chiefs deployed agents of magical power for social control, obviously, as with the renowned case of the Papuan hinterland Mekeo, only "the domestic sorcerer" (*ungaunga*) and not "the war magician" (*fai'a*) was deferred to as the means of requiting *internal* malcontents, and in this role complemented physical punishments rather than fighting (Trompf 2008a: 75–76). When peacemaking is ritualized among the Wahgi, *both* the sorcerer/magician and the war magician take turns to play their parts, the first and the second bespelling the least edible, hardest bananas (see Figure 8) to signal how arduous it is to stop war (OTs: J. Kai et al. 1976)! Among the New Guinea highland Maring, still further inland, specialists in magic always monitor the edges of war and peace, pigs' blood being ritually rubbed on the 'fighting stones' (*bamp ku*) to mark the time of conflict's arrival; and the stones' post-war removal into seclusion, after all obligations to allies and deceased warriors' close kin have been met, allows prohibited meats to be eaten again and pig herds to be well fed for the touted promise of great feasting in years to come (Rappaport 1967: 23–24). The magico-spiritual very frequently *serves* violence, even if often not entailing overt physical hurt in its ritual exertions.

---

[28]  OT: Koroti Kosi, paramount chief, Lese Oalai, May 1974 (Toaripi-Moripi [far eastern Elema cultural complex, Papuan Gulf] case as very typical).

Figure 8 Wahgi war magician bespelling barely edible bananas at a peace ceremony, New Guinea highlands. *Photo: by the author.*

Issues of sorcery and witchcraft, however, conduct us directly to issues of socio-religious change.

## 2.3 A Diachronic Approach

As noted before, when most ethnological investigators entered the field they sought to document a traditional society as they experienced it, usually without oral- or ethno-historical training or encouragement to develop an historical perspective. But of course, after missionary and pacificatory effects, they usually had security from any attack themselves and, even if choosing to record data from a place least touched by pressures for *gutpela sindaun* (PNG tok pisin: 'sitting down in peace') (Mombi 2019: 7–30), they could still easily miss the nervous intensity of 'the old time' and undetectable influences of 'the new' (Tomasetti 1976). To avoid misassessments, one requires sensitivity towards unexpected pressures on custom (*kastom*) in contact and post-contact contexts. Considering these diachronic issues, we will first see how they apply in Melanesia's south-western Pacific provenance and then look to the wider Pacific where their relevance looms much greater.

## 2.3.1 Melanesia

When the stopper is placed on the inviolable principles and actions of avengement, whether by fear of a colonial administration's punition of 'wild justice' or Christian sacro-pastoral prohibitions against killing, one should expect different kinds of diffusions in payback energies. Bottling up warrior energy and then sudden outbursts of vicious rage can be one resulting problematic. The Papuan Highland Tauade present an important case, after Anglo-Canadian anthropologist Christopher Hallpike's field-work among them in the 1970s, when he explained (1977: 40, 80–81) their propensity for homicidal violence as a 'Heraclitean' passion to 'kill for the sake of killing', without recognizing that males in an already relatively volatile society showed symptoms of severe stress from a shutting down of their old system. Frustration over less fighting, moreover, could bring on predatory quests to rape, offensive seductions and mistreatment of women, or even homoerotic exploits instead of club-smashing an enemy victim's skull and releasing the semen believed to reside in the head (as recent work on an Iqwaye leader indicates) (Mimica 2007: 80–83). Where cannibalism had been previously focused on more distant others, its persistence under social pressures could turn inward enough to threaten a whole language group's existence, as Margaret Mead ([1935] 1950: 109) alleged of the Mundugunmur on the Yuat River (middle Sepik region).[29] Variations of strategy to manage incoming pressures were innumerable. Initiations to

---

[29] Note that linguists now treat Biwat and Mundugumor as distinct though related languages, and Mead's 'language group' means both.

help handle fear in war were often shortened. The Hunjara (in the wider Orokaiva grouping) wisely replaced ritual homicide of an enemy with pig slaughter (Chinnery 1919: 39; cf. Iteanu 1990); the Sepik Iatmül ceased headhunting raids on the vulnerable, female-led Tchambuli (Chambri Lakes), taking instead a few captives and ritually killing them back home (Mead [1935] 1950: 107). Other symptomatic changes near contact would be higher sorcery accusations, arising from the results of introduced disease-bearing germs (see n. 14), which could spread inland and adversely affect tribal dynamics even before foreigners got beyond the coasts (Hughes 1977: 107).

When, under mission or colonial pressure, long-inured and culture-specific taboos and rules were actually thrown off, the trauma involved could spark conflict, as on Atchin (off Malekula, Vanuatu), when encouragement in the 1930s to abandon the custom of a daughter marrying her grandfather if her father was killed (or died) sparked terrible conflict across the islet (Layard 1942: 125). With external pressures to stop tribal fighting, new patterns of violent reprisal arose. Instead of full-scale raiding, individual revenge killings occurred, still commonly indiscriminate yet increasingly on pre-selected 'culprits' – as among the Bena, with 'payback running' becoming more important as a recourse after the Australian administration proscribed open war. Among the Kaluli (or Mount Bosavi area, Southern Highlands, Papua), when open fighting was blocked in the 1950s, witch-sorcery, previously less feared for being among peoples afar off, was now believed to derive from among neighbouring groups. Unobtrusive anti-sorcery raids (*sei sandam*) became popular against specific harm-workers, and groups among whom sorcerers were identified and killed were as interested as accusers to see the colour of the alleged *sei*'s heart when ritually extracted. If discoloured, the *sei*'s clan would give compensation; if not, a false accusation had occurred and hostilities, whether new or traditional, followed (Schieffelin 1990: 12–13, 58–59, 78, 101–109). Missions were at the forefront of new settlement patterns across the Melanesian board: lineages in dispersed (smaller) hamlets were encouraged into (bigger) villages. Practising sorcerers from the outside now became potential 'enemies within'. Some villages, such as the thousand-strong Ilahita settlement (Ilahita Arapesh), grew because traditionalists shored up their defences against the new pressures for change, and an augmented cult of Nggwal used assault sorcery for social control (Tuzin 1976: 99–101, 117–145); while in the large 300-strong Massim mountain village of Kalauna on Goodenough Island (Papua), sorcery imputations became a problem issue barely known in smaller settlements, and even emergent Christian leaders have had to play on the fear of sorcery power to maintain clout (Young 1971: 89–93). The general case, especially in coastal Melanesia, moreover, is that, even if war and murder cease, 'localities keep their old barriers', and sorcery and witchcraft remain to shore up defences believed necessary (Fortune [1932] 1963: 30). All such shifts have to be taken into account in field research, and purely synchronic analysis would be insufficient for explaining both the presence and varying levels of violence within Melanesian contexts where pre-contact mentalities recognizably persist.

Sorcery (not often expressed by actual violent physical harming, please remember) is a crucial litmus test for socio-religious change as the region absorbs contact, Christianization and modernity. Early foreign settlements and plantations on the coast involved 'population displacements' further inland, and in some areas, as among the Rawa (lower Ramu River, Madang), this 'set off a series of vicious local wars' in which 'sorcery likewise became extreme and severe', and epidemics resulting from contact made a 'rich seed-bed' for sorcery accusations (as among the hinterland Madang Garia) (Dalton 2007: 43; Lawrence 1984: 26; see also Knauft 1976 on the Gebusi).[30] If traditionally revenge or redress activity was so typically expressed in open warring deeds, and these had to be foregone under both newly imposed colonial laws (against murder and disorder) and mission talk of relevant Commandments ('not to kill' and 'to love one another', from the Old and New Testaments), the repression of negative payback impetuses saw them narrowed into covert procedures. In consequence, traditional leadership (i.e., in its chiefly and managerial guises) was inevitably undermined, first because it had depended on the ethos of military prowess and second because indigenous appointees for the offices of administration and

---

[30] Note also how dysentery connected to explorers' first contact with the Bokondini Dani (in the Baliem Valley, 1938) made for fear of the whites' return after their earlier appearances: Ploeg (1995: 227–239).

church were often from fresh blood, newly educated and linguistically skilled for a different order. Sorcerers, however, could increase in influence, if in secret, as an alien, loose, insidious factor, often in settlement outskirts as a 'non-reciprocal man' (Burridge 1965: 232–236; 1975: 95–102). What has been called 'sacred revenge' became, in a sense, more sacred for being handled 'spiritually' (Stewart and Strathern 2019: 18), the last bastion of negative reciprocity in traditional religion operating more surreptitiously (as has happened the world round). And it usually left villagers who embraced post-contact change with a tragic uncertainty over promised blessings of life, or left grassroots leaders who could combine old and new power elements little choice but to manipulate 'spiritual harm-dealers' for the changed situation. If anything of the old laws was to remain unscathed, with no traditional 'judgment to protect the oppressed and no punishment for the oppressor', headmen had 'to replace objective jurisprudence' by following 'the treacherous path of sorcery', as missionary ethnologist Josef Meier conceded early on for the Tolai (Meier 1913: 2–3).

This is only to scratch the surface of a long and complex story that needs to be better filled out in a companion Element about socio-religious change. Suffice it to say here that growing anxieties about sorcery and witchcraft close at hand and within what is supposed to be a trusted security circle have been exacerbated by post-contact social change and modernization. Both Mission and Administration discouraged isolated hamlets and fostered 'the village model' (let alone market townships) after the image of an ordered European countryside, without pre-knowledge of inimical new health problems and intra-community tensions resulting.[31] In the longer distant past, payback killing for sorcery was generally indiscriminate, and, if you ever made such an important man as a sorcerer your successful target, that was a lucky outcome or daring deed indeed. While witch torture and burning was known in traditional Africa (Maraves), pre-Columbian Middle America (Aztecs) and Indian tribal settings (Bihls), in Melanesia it was, exceptions aside, more a matter of witches being notoriously elusive

[31] For Melanesia, the most thoughtful recognition of this is Bennett (1974: 31, 42, 120, etc.) (Weather Cost Guadalcanal); for the wider world, Ranger (1992: 213–214).

(in the imagination above all) or exiled as wives likely to be manipulated by spirits or foes (yet to places where they became 'fair game' or tended to suicide).[32] But distortions of tradition – social pathologies due to fears and accusations, the pressures for sorcery drives or divination rituals, the killing of alleged witches – needs commentary and diachronic analysis in another, companion Element to this, as do many more recent changes in expressions of violence in armed conflict, punitive action and social relations.

The diachronic approach – or historical attention to long-term change – we shall now find is crucial for what we will now write about that is relevant from wider Oceania.

### 2.3.2 Micronesia and Polynesia

If it seems strange that we have refrained from considering Micronesian and Polynesian patterns of traditional violence except under this diachronic rubric, the quandary is simply resolved. Documentation of war in the wider Pacific is overwhelmingly mixed in with the embroilment of foreigners in the conflict, whether the intruders actually made war against resisting Indigenes or intruded in on their pre-existing conflicts. The time factor is also obviously involved here. Relatively speaking, wider Pacific Islander cultures are reported upon much earlier than those of the 'Black Islands', so the plotting of prolonged change and outside influence diachronologically is critical for establishing 'traditional ways'.

### 2.3.2.1 Warfare

We can take first some examples from Micronesia, and they will immediately highlight diachronic considerations because serious interaction with the outside world in the wider Oceania occurred so much earlier than in Melanesia. Enduring Chamorro traditions (from Guam and the northern Marianas) have it that war was between competing chiefdoms (each village

---

[32] On (pre-contact) witch executions and heart-removal, see, for example, Kelly (1993: 249–294) (Etoro, Papuan Plateau); on traditional-looking claims of leaders' success in killing witches, see, for example, Kuehling (2014: 277b); cf., Fortune ([1932] 1963: 129) (Dobu); cf. Trompf (2008a, esp. 63) (Wahgi) with P. Stewart, personal communication, 2021 (Duna).

chief or *maga'lahi* ('first born') laying claim to seniority genealogically, back to the earliest (or founder) chiefs. And if few lives were taken in fighting, it was kept incessant, above all by warriors whose family had lost nobility and prestigious land through misdemeanour or arrogance (the free-floating *acha'ot* grouping) and who desperately wanted to regain 'high caste' (or *matao/matua*) status. Already we can see what is characteristic of wider Pacific social orders: their hierarchization according to 'ramages', the leader first arriving on an island being the first chief bequeathing the highest level of seniority to his first descendant, and others ranked (whether patri- or matrilineally) in decreasing clout, indeed a lessened effective spiritual empowering (often called *mana*) according to this descent principle. 'The first canoe' also typically symbolized the distinction between (chief-bred) nobles and commoners, whether the latter were already attendants on a voyage-venture or the conquered prior inhabitants of an island taken. In the Chamorro case, the free accumulation of wives by high chiefs (whose power was sacrosanct and arbitrary) meant that women could cross 'caste' boundaries and play a role in a chief's council, even advising on levels of punishment (with respect to offences, women were never to blame, and the men were left with full responsibility) (Cunningham 1992: 168, 179–181, 186–187; with Petersen 2009; cf. Firth 1957: esp. 371; Sahlins 1958: 141–142; Feinberg 1988: 11–27; Hage and Harary 1996: 22–50).

Still, relevant primary-source materials going back to sixteenth- and seventeenth-century contact situations for the Chamorros are expectedly few, and the war chants that have been passed down belong to the context of wars against the Spanish in Guam (starting 1671). The songs – meant to stand like 'a[n ancestrally charged] house post' and like 'basalt rock' – were mnemonically repeated by religious specialists (such as shaman-wizards or *makåhna*s) who imbibed them into fighters to guarantee victory. We know from early missionary sources that sorcerers (*ka'kåhna*s, in other words, '*mana*-possessors' or war magicians) saw to it that ancestral skulls were borne into battle by warriors, who displayed them before fighting and set them in their protective defence trenches as final protectors (thus rather humbly accepting their defeats by the Spanish as willed by their dead, since the Europeans freely trampled on the so-deposited skulls in their flush of triumph) (García [1683] 2004: 173–176; Farrar and Sellmann 2016; 133–

140).[33] Here we should start being aware of functionaries (normally high-caste) used by chiefs to enshroud warfare with advice on tactics (fortifications, war canoes), special rules (such as the prohibition of barbed weapons by the Chamorro) and ritual procedures, even the formal lining-up of enthused and decorated braves, fiercely chanting towards the foe. Micronesian and Polynesian warfare tends to have more formality (even 'etiquette') about it, with warrior nobles, primed by combative sport between fights, typically seeking to dominate military action for prestige purposes, and in some cultures with powerful women ready for involvement if men in their high-caste families had been lost (particularly in the eastern Polynesian Marquesas) (Petersen 2009: 158–211; Gunson 1987; Thomas 1990; cf. Earle 1997: 131–142).

Most of our information about war in the wider Pacific, to reiterate, comes from within a context of decidedly outside interference. To inform more about Micronesia, consider the remarkable case of the Palau (Pelew) island complex, first made known to the wider world by the English free-booting mariner Francis Drake (1579). After missionary failures and hasty visitations, it became better known that an internal war had long been raging between two tribal confederations headed by two contesting paramount chiefs, one centered at Koror in the southern group and one at Babeldaob to the north-west of the big island of Melekeok. This will help clarify for readers whether intertribal fighting went on when islands were small. Remarkably, single small islands were often divided down the middle; and if they were united it was because an enemy was chased to another nearby island, attacks then necessarily involving canoes. From 1783, British traders unashamedly fed this Palauan conflict by combining innocuous exchange with the introduction of muskets – and sometimes mariners on short loan to fire them in war. Fighting was so exacerbated (and *un*traditionally bloody) and the situation so tainted (influenza also striking after further trading efforts) that exasperated representatives of the British navy blew up fourteen 'clubhouses' (for warriors' meetings, including

---

[33] Note that prior missionary destruction of sacred skulls to mark conversion was obviously resented and contributed to hostilities for undermining *ka'khana* power.

access to cult prostitutes) and extracted an on-board treaty from the chiefs to cease armed strife and headhunting (1883). The history of comparable interferences elsewhere in Micronesia make for the same difficulties in reconstructing religious aspects of traditional war. We learn that, in the Marshall Islands, enemy tribes sought to destroy as much of other side's property as they could, and in 1883 on Arno atoll, when traders saw their copra assets endangered, they sold muskets to try salvaging them, only to find themselves dodging bullets 'from the rifles they themselves supplied' in a battle quite unheard of before in such an isolated place (Hezel 1983: 66–74, 272–281, 293–294; cf. Alaima Talu et al., 1979: 44–95).

Actually, being a trader, a long-distant voyager, or even an explorer does not always provide the best vantage point for documenting violence, because one is forever hoping for a safe haven. So we will have accounts of visitors anchoring away from trouble and thus missing action, or else almost inevitably causing disturbance that will disrupt pre-contact arrangements. Even the close passing of Spanish galleons by Easter Island/Rapanui in the seventeenth century, I have argued, set in train sudden hopes for social transformation, as attested by the haphazard and non-traditional placement of over forty-five statues at the island's quarry (Rano Raraku) facing out to sea, with drawn-out intra-island strife then following from those no longer wanting subjection as *moai*-carvers (into the 1810s, when, after the real presence of Europeans, the formally arranged statues of the great ancestors [cf. 1.1] were overturned) (Trompf 2002: 457–464, with Owsley et al. 2016; cf. Diamond 2005: 93–112 [with caution]). For other examples, the Avarua tribe was decimated and banished for seven years to western Rarotonga (Cook Islands), after their jealous role in the 1814 fracas with the *Cumberland*'s sandalwood-seekers, while, on overpopulated Tongareva atoll (Penrhyn, Cook Islands), occasional outsider presence inspired an unusual tribal alliance in a great revenge surge against the hated Tautuans, almost wiping them out in 1853 (Maude 1968: 351, 353, 355; Hiroa/Buck 1932: 55–56, and see Section 2.1 in this Element). We have moved to Polynesian cases, remembering that both Micronesia and Polynesia are overwhelmingly Austronesian-speaking and highly related cultural complexes, though together carrying only 22 per cent of the discrete linguo-religious traditions known across the Pacific Islands.

A common feature in Polynesian cosmologies is the cluster of department-mental gods, most readers perhaps remembering the 'core' Maori myth of the arduous primal separation of Sky (Rangi) and Earth (Papatuanuku) from their procreative embrace. Among their offspring prising them apart, we find Tumatauenga (or Tu), the angry-faced one who believed only killing his parents would achieve their momentous *Trennung*; and he became honoured *across* tribes as 'the god and father of fierce human beings', to whom the first enemy slain in a battle was offered (Grey [1855] 1929: 5). Where intergroup fighting was intense, we can expect gods of war to rise in legitimating authority. On Mangaia (south Cooks), the most victorious chief was held to possess the most 'ruling power' (*mangaia*) through the god of war, Rongo, whose cult, dominated by two high priests, 'transcended clan boundaries' and waited things out in neu-trality during war, nervous of being deposed if having seemed previously ill-disposed to the victor (Siikala 1992: 116). When we find war earliest documented for Polynesia, however, outside forces have already affected it, including with modern weaponry.

When in 1796 there arrived in Tahiti the mixed Protestant personnel from the London Missionary Society (LMS), the locals already had firearms and were embroiled in their own 'dynastic wars' between high chiefs, apparently the most entrenched one being in the so-called 'Leeward' or western island group (Borabora and Taha'a versus Huahine and Ra'iatea). From their base in the Matavai district on the northern side of Tahiti Is. proper, the favour of the LMS missionaries was cultivated by a high chief pretending to paramountcy over the eastern or 'Windward' group, one Tu (II, later King Pomare II). But Tu's family derived far to the east from the Tuamotu island group, and his claims had been sorely tested in war since the 1760s by traditionally senior ramages in Tahiti's west and south-west. Under the cult of the war god 'Oro, who was becoming more prominent in immediate pre-contact times, competing claims to the highest role were preferably settled by negotiation, with a great deal of aristocratic rhetorical bluff, but in this case wars kept erupting, with old weaponry mixed with new (the latter substantially introduced by the famous mutineers of the *Bounty*). Both sides kept grasping for the highest symbols of power, especially the main 'Oro idol, traditionalists fighting 'to restore the ancient form of government to the island' (but not without the new arms) and opposing Tu's arrogance for abetting change, since he sought the missionaries' support (apparently identifying their Jehovah with the downplayed Tahitian Creator Ta'aroa) and opened a lucrative, monopolistic pork trade with New South Wales.[34]

Through all this we can detect features of traditional war that were fairly indicative of wider Polynesia. The units of war were larger than in Melanesia and Micronesia: a good deal of diplomatic toing and froing went on between chiefly centres to discover who was allied to whom or not in any particular situation. A royal or paramount chief might travel to secure an alliance and could expect gifts, especially of woven grass-reed or beaten-bark (*tapa*) mats, and if a noticeably lessened amount or a failure of any negotiating party to turn up signalled half-heartedness or even insult, calls to arms followed. Insults or breaching principles of honour – between high-ranked figures – triggered most serious fighting, because wars were mostly conceived as between great chiefly families, often competing for ramage superiority (see Section 2.3.2.1 and n. 42). Royals and high-chiefly family members deployed nobles (*ari'i, arioi, ariki* or cognates), not uncommonly including strong women (even queens) and (noble-born) priests and prophets, to constitute a warrior force, retaining any commoners they might choose for military occasions. Noble warriors were frequently of very strong build, benefiting from the flow of food gifts up from the commoners to the nobility by sumptuary privilege. Warriors had to handle both sea and land. In cases where attacks and invasions came from the sea, the vessels deployed were sometimes capable of taking up to 100 armed warriors: on

[34] For relevant unpublished material, G. Pratt, 'LMS South Sea Journal', 18 July 1832 (LMS/CWM Archives, SOAS, University of London, Ms Box 6) (Leewards); J. Jefferson, 'LMS South Sea Journal', 1801 (LMS/CWM Arch. Box 3) (quotation); and then Adams (1901) (highest claims); Barrow (1980: 104–106) (Bounty mutineers, 1789, after engaged themselves within tribal war on Tubuai Is. [now French Polynesia]); King (2011: 127, pl. 190) (King Pomare I's wrapped-up wickerwork image of 'Oro); Siikala (1992: 214–225) (vicissitudes in war and relations); Gunson (1969: 71–72 [Pomare's monopoly], 73, 78–81 [anti-'Oro, pro-Jehovah (for Pomare = Creator Ta'aroa)]).

explorer Captain James Cook's estimate, one among the 160 double canoes he viewed (1769) measured 108 feet in length, longer than the renowned *Endeavour*, most carrying their own supportive 'god houses', and with over 300 large war vessels said to ply Tahitian waters. Beaches, in contrast to Melanesian fight-fields, were favoured places for battle, with bones of foes left on the sand to make joy of victory or sadness of loss, and with the trophies of human jaw-bones quickly hung up (sometimes on small carved boats) to greet enemies who dared coming back to their long-house after plundering victors had gone home (Cook 1821: vol. 1, 170, 252–253;[35] with Oliver 2002: 145–155; Kuschel 1998; Gunson 1987; Sears 1998: Reilly 2001). As in New Guinea, we can find abstention from sex before fighting, usage of war stones and magical preparations: on Niue, warriors kept themselves apart for three days not far from the likely battle-site or take-off point, wore three sacred stones and *fuo polo* berries held in a plaited girdle around their midriffs, blackened their spears, and joined in curses and a war dance under the supervision of a *taula-atua* or war shaman (Loeb 1978: 131–133).

Yes, religious specialists were involved in military operations. For the Tahitian case, priests as 'men of knowledge' (like Tupai'a, who was enlisted to accompany Cook) were navigators and war-canoe commanders (Driessen 2005), while also protecting the 'god-houses' (mostly for 'Oro) set on the vessels' decks, and even wearing mourning dress (*heva*), with shimmering feathered headdress, to underscore the quest for retribution (Figure 9). Human sacrifice of kept, enslaved prisoners (or chosen malefactors) bolstered spiritual energy in the ethos: before the missionaries came, at the great stone platform (*marae*) dedicated to 'Oro (then as "the Supreme Being") at Matavai, Cook just missed seeing the 'beating' of the victims' skulls with the high priest's maces 'till they were dead' (in 1777) (Cook 1821: vol. 3, 194; 1961: vol. 2, 401).[36]

---

[35] Defer also to W. A. Hodges, 'The Fleet of Otaheite assembled at Oparee' (crayon drawing, fin. 1777 [British Museum it. 1940,0810.17]), the basis for Figure 9.

[36] Note the etching by W. Woolett, 'Human Sacrifice in a Moral in Otaheite' (Tahiti, occurring to the beat of a drum, those presenting holding forks for [compensatory?] funerary cannibalism, with wrapped deceased *ari'i* placed on a

Figure 9 Depicted fleet of Tahitian war canoes, witnessed 1769. *Photo: W. A. Hodges (orig. crayon), 1777 (British Museum).*

A statistically based point of distinction has been recently made that more hierarchical societies tend to engage in human sacrifice (Watts et al. 2015; cf. Babadzan 1993). With chieftainships more equally poised in rivalry, it was less in evidence in Samoa (and relegated into myth) (Cain 1979: 388–389) while being notable under virtual monarchies. Following Valerio Valeri's groundbreaking study of Hawai'i, *Kingship and Sacrifice* (1985a), when the great open-air Temple is refreshed, in the annual *Luakini* festival, the finale entailed the king offering an immense sacrifice to the gods – many pigs, fish, bananas, coconuts, *oloa* cloths and, yes, a few humans (typically enemies or descendants of defeated kings or well-remembered

*marae*, apparently next to dispatched enemies' trophy-skulls) (London, 1784). For god-houses in art, eyewitness paintings of them, one even before Cook for Cpt. James Wallis, 1767, see Oliver (2019: 905 with figs. 26.1, 29.5, at [pp.] 1216, 1275).

transgressors), from which celebration food distribution went down to the 'little people' or needy (Valeri 1985a: 69, 141, 229, 309–311 et passim; cf. Ellis 1842: vol. 4, 161; Kolb and Dixon 2002), On Tonga, when the most sacred chief-king (or *Tu'i Tonga*, of Tongatapu Island) had died, it was up to the next highest royal, often the queen acting in a priestly role, to decide whether offering a human sacrifice was required.[37] Back to Tahiti's case, priests were numerous among both nobles and commoners, yet each only served their own kind, sustaining warrior life down to funerals, with the great deceased ones, after prolonged mourning, sent into soul-flight from their places of wrapping on the *marae*, to resecure their privileged enjoyments in the after-world. Priests who performed pre-conflict chant-prayers also usually doubled as sorcerers protecting against enemies, debilitating them by 'snatching their souls'. Prophets who predicted the outcome of battle, with oracular force and augury, came from both 'castes', and occasionally renowned commoners could join courtly circles. Non-priestly nobles had roles as mediators and advisors, though dictating punishment, especially death (by head-bashing) or being forced to walk (barefoot) on a reef for treasonable offences, belonged to the highest ruler or high chiefs.[38] A Marquesan chief would foster ascetic specialists for sanctioning malcontents: they sickened a victim by burying sweat or urine stains on stolen cloth under their altars, killing when required by dropping these leavings with heavy wood in deep seas (Robarts [1806] 1974: 254–255). Priesthoods were fundamental for Micronesian traditional life (Hezel and Dobbin 2011), though they have been rare in Melanesia, the lakeside Sentani (in the hinterland north of West Papua) making for a special exception in distinguishing priests for their mediation in conflict, curing wounds, foretelling

---

[37] J. Thomas, 'Mythology of the Tongans' (MS, Wesleyan Methodist Missionary Society Papers, SOAS), London, [1870s], 256, discussed by Cummins (1977: 73). Compare queen-like Salamâsina on Samoa, Schoeffel (1987).

[38] Oliver (2019: 65–95 [priests], 71–75 [on sorcerers' use of empowering and protective *ti'i* spirit figures]); Badadzan 1993: 34–38, 82–88 (sorcerer-priests); N. Gunson (1962: 208, 210–211, 233, 235, with 221, 236 on punishments); Hiroa/ Buck (1936: 13 et passim) (on snaring souls by using gods/spirits and keeping them as familiars for further use to protect the group; and Tahiti as 'central').

weather, or mortuary and even chiefly functions (Kamma 1975: 51–55, 65–67).

In the morass of diary accounts of attacks on Europeans and of missionary reports about receding traditional war practice, we can pick up some interesting details, with the extent of rounded information from any one island complex depending on the pace and degree of irruption brought by foreigners and on whether old ways stood better preserved in less disturbed contexts. We can detect how ritual and ethico-regulatory prescriptions affected levels of violence. When Cook's ships *Resolution* and *Discovery* anchored in Kealakekua Bay (great Hawai'i Island) in January 1779, for example, where a crucial royal temple (*heiau*) and chiefly funerary platform (*morai*) were located, and near where royals were secretly buried above the cliffs of Keôua, the season of harvest celebration and of attention to Lono, god of fertility, was ending. Though highly honoured (perhaps by some as Lono himself), Cook pressed too much for shipping timber from the sacred site. Significantly, when he had to return in February because of squalls, the season of Kû (or Kûka'ilimoku), god of war, had been ushered in (with its human sacrifices). Souring reactions towards Cook, particularly with his surreptitious attempt to kidnap the island king Kalani'iopu'u, soon caused warriors to storm in anger, the great discoverer being ironically despatched with a steel blade already traded by one of his crew. The wet season divided times of relative peace and war, and young noble warriors would have been training themselves under the very same unpredictable weather conditions that brought Cook's ships back to the bay. Collective spectator feelings in watching the 'sportive' sparring of individuals (also popular in Tonga) would have been high (see Figure 10). Besides, even Cook's arrogant appropriating of materials, his theft, would have been interpreted as 'a form of violence' (Thomas 2003: 378–406; Williams 2008; Wilkes 2019: 144–191, esp. 144).[39]

---

[39] In 'consolidated' Hawai'ian tradition, however, Cook is Lono: Kamakau (1991: 53–54). On fluidities in the meanings of war and uses of force before unification processes in Hawai'i, see D'Arcy (2018: 49–108) (firearms entering the picture from 1786).

Figure 10 Depicted sparring in single combat: sportive warriors practising as spectacle, Tonga, *ca.* 1777. *Photo: E. Germer (1965) for Museum für Völkerkunde Leipzig.*

In different contexts we find other noteworthy protocols, principles of honour and consensus standards pertaining to fighting. In Tonga, famously, the sacred rulers *Tuʻi Tonga*s transcended military activities, with their seat always on eastern Tongatapu at the ancient capital of Muʻa, the site of the monumental royal tombs, yet near where the great canoes would embark to forge and control the maritime empire. He could arbitrate between chiefly conflicts and supervise 'semi-feudalized' land holdings (Goldman 1955: 686), and his sanctity did still rely on a legacy of great warriorhood, justifying his deployment of the lesser and 'secular' warlord chiefs near him to control Tongapu itself. As the great 'fertilizer' of Tongan strength or embodiment of *mana*, he received first-fruit harvest offerings from all other chiefly families at the spectacular annual *'Inasi* (first-fruits tribute) ceremony; as 'descendant' from Tangaloa (the sky deity highest in the pantheon) and thus mediating for all deities, he also officiated with his priesthood at the funerals of slain mighty ones, to ensure their safe passage to the sky islands (*langi*) above, with his own death made special by the strangulation of his wives (Mariner in Martin [1818] 1827: esp. vol. 1, 199–248; vol. 2, 68).

Already during Cook's prolonged stay (in 1777), though, eight centuries of genealogical recording and sacrosanctity surrounding the *Tu'i Tonga* seemed in jeopardy: Cook witnessed a father and son taking the office jointly, a sign of anxious insurance (Bott 1982: 19–37; Clunie 2013: 161–162). At the time of Wesleyan missionary influence (from 1822), moreover, the Tongan imperial aegis had weakened, especially over their old expansionist rival Samoa (whose divinities and society were less hierarchic and now divided between confederacies of independent chiefdoms) (Krämer 1902–1903; Cain 1979: 144–464; Siikala 1992: 178–191), and a battle raged between the secular high chiefs of the two north-eastern Tongan groups of Ha'apai and Vava'u. These chiefs were holders of real or coercive power, with new military techniques being picked up from Fiji. The Wesleyans found themselves welcomed by the impressive Taufa'ahau, lord over the scattered Ha'apai islets, who defeated his main rival (not with traditional weapons only), and, since the presiding *Tu'i Tonga* Laufilitonga also overreached his sacred role into military affairs, Taufa'ahau followed Wesleyan promptings to usurp the sacred office, declaring himself King George (Tupoi I) at his baptism in 1831, to rule a Christian kingdom that could avoid European colonial annexation (Gifford 1929: 298–332; Siikala 1992: 153–158). Before baptism Taufa'ahau dishonoured the gods, and – seeing his smashing the sacra of his tutelary deity Taufa'itahi had no ill effects, nor even the murder of his oldest priestess – he decided the old religion as a whole lacked true *mana*. An internal Tongan peace was secured, with the tension over the flouting of previously inviolable tradition being eased when the *Tu'i Tonga*'s family fell under the protection of the Catholics and their competing mission (in place by 1842). Peaceful rule followed, although there remained loose ends in the far island reaches of Tongan influence (Van der Grijp 2014: 108).

On Mangaia (Cooks), where we have seen two war-god high priests neutral vis-à-vis fighting (like the *Tu'i Tonga*), detailed reconstruction of engagement rules has been easier, as missionary records show. When not used, for some important snippets, weapons were placed in a scaffolding (*'ata*) dedicated to Tongaiti, who (as one of the sons of the Vatea, father of the gods, in myth) was given supervision over artefacts of war, at least for the powerful Turanga tribe. Spears and clubs were made of ironwood, almost as hard as metal and taking months to carve, with other instruments being shields, flat wooden swords and stones. A human was sacrificed before battle as propitiation to 'Oro, the war cry to 'split 'Oro's coconut!' (*va'ite 'akari a Rongo*! or the enemy's head) went up, and divination outcomes were assessed, as when the chief of the war party inspected two turbo shells left on his tribal *marae* overnight to see which one had fallen, if ever so slightly. As a formality, the ground of the fighting had been selected and relayed to the opposition, the chosen spot cleared of as many obstacles as possible, and the war party (*tutai*) went in formation, senior warriors of the patrilineage most involved before two other layers of lesser age groups. Focus on the field could be on two leaders, one aggrieved and seeking revenge on the other almost in a personal duel, and wives of chiefs might join in furiously if they saw a threat to their prestigious husbands. This was a war (*miro*) called *tatemu* (only to kill leaders) as against exterminating as many as possible (*tu'uri karai'i*), relatives included, with warriors of either type having confidence that by death they could enter *Tiari*, a Valhalla of constant dancing, even with previous combatants, much preferred to the 'Oven of Miru' farthest below in the earth. Fate in the latter would apply to a man who killed a relative in peace rather than war, an act that incurred 'the blood curse', enabling an enemy group to come to despatch the culprit in a mock battle, with those normally his comrades, though armed, not taking action to defend him (Hiroa/Buck 1934: 156–161, 165).[40]

To reiterate my argument elsewhere, traditional Polynesian (and most other Austronesian cosmologies) were typically vertical, with the sky- and

---

[40] Using especially John Williams and Wyatt Gill (LMS), and see on the apparent layering of the warriors' paradise (also named Poëpoê) Maretu (1880) 1983: 111 (with Gill). For a comparable if atypical heaven/hell conceptualization, with a skyward Valhalla-like 'red place' for warriors and supportive wives to keep on exercising their vital ways and an earthy 'brown' one for the cowardly and unworthy, see Trompf (2008a: 150) (on the Southern highland Erave).

upper-world-connected deities above the earth and with the underworld-
and death-associated forces below. Popular myth-legends across the islands
have handsome Maui, a demi-god, fire-bringing culture-hero and trickster
figure, pushing up the sky so that it would not be so suffocating for people
(Tonga), or drawing up islands to the surface of the sea with his fishhook
(Hawai'i), or dying in an effort to find his father and defeat death in the
underworld, by changing into a worm to enter the vagina of Hine-nui-te-
pô, goddess of death (Maori) (Westervelt [1910] 2010: 31–55; Pomare and
Cowan 1930: vol. 1, 14–20; cf. Goldman 1970). If sometimes tempered by
talk of reaching the far horizon, the narratives reflect not only an up-down
orientation, but the likely priority of the superior god(s) being highest, and
the after-world ideal (at least as projected by priests) for the nobility being
skyward. With the increased prominence of war gods, however, sights were
apparently set lower. Mangaia's Rongo, for instance, dwelt in the underworld (*atua po*) and Tahiti's 'Oro in the center of the earth, and warriors'
post-mortem enjoyments consequently imaged in their vicinity; although
admittedly the sense of verticality still held, with 'Oro as rider of the
rainbow between the above and below (Hiroa/Buck 1934: 161–162).[41] In
Hawai'i, as the legends of 'Umi, conqueror of Maui Is. (*ca.* 1500) have it, the
king necessarily participated in less elevated divinities of the Wild
(Haku'ôhi'a) in his initiation and War (Kûkâ'ilimoku) in his initial status,
because he came from his royal father's union with a commoner ('dirty
one') and usurped his father's inactive firstborn through military prowess, a
warning for rulers in the future that more ethereal and core-lineage or
senior-ramage connections may not always be enough to secure succession

---

[41] See T[euira] Henry (1928: 120–121, 129–130) on the coming of the 'Oro cult to
Tahiti not long before contact and his special, newly sanctioning patronage of the
*Arioi* or nobles; compare Oliver (2019: 881–964). On the relativities of commoner
expectations of afterlife conditions, note how whereas the Tongan nobility were
expected to live as stars, ordinary folk, treated cruelly by them as worthless,
could only expect to live as vermin under the ground, even if their graves were
nurturing the earth (*fonua*); one important reason for the acceptance of the
Christian message: Trompf (2008): vol. 2, 1288;Martin/Mariner (1827): esp. vol.
1, 68; vol. 2, 93–123.

in a warrior's world (priestly traditions recording over twenty-five signifi-cant tribal and inter-island battles before unification by 1810) (Valeri 1985b: 90–98; cf. 1982).[42]

Looking south to New Zealand, cosmological reflection shows some adjustment to the huge spread and location of 'the land of the long white cloud' (Aotearoa, referring at first only to the North Island) and to its towering snow-capped mountains, each region accepting one peak as sacred and inviolable to approach (*tapu*). Rûaumoko the volcano god was typically held to remain in the womb of his (earth-)mother Papa, as when, in the key myth, Sky and Earth had not yet separated, so that his tantrums make for eruptions, his spasms and disturbing quiescence connect to death (as in childbirth), and his strong internal movements to turn over his mother produce the oscillation of hot and cold seasons not known elsewhere in the Pacific Islands. In the divine affairs of Aotearoa, the great struggles between the gods signified the heavens to be a crucial means of escape (White 1887: vol. 1, 17–112; Best 1924: 95). When humans are afoot, erupting conflicts involved many more tribal groups (*iwi*) and *hapuu* (sub-tribes or clans) in interaction and in alliance relationships than elsewhere in Oceania, and greater complexity in territorial occupancy, from small islands to inland holdings without a coastline.

We do have various tidbits that help reconstruct special pre-contact aspects of Maori warfare. The keeping of narratives of warrior exploits by priest-specialists (*tohunga*) are precious survivals of shared morale (Dittner 1907: 100–120), as are *haka* rituals of collective dance, tattooed facial changes and sung poetry preliminary to battle (some interestingly invoking Rûaumoko) (Merrett in Binney 2007: 37, illustr. 3.4; Simmons 2003: 5; cf. Orbell 1996: 129), and the exchange of chanted greetings when 'pilgrims of Tû [the war god]' or warriors returning from a campaign are welcomed by a

---

[42] In both Micronesia and Polynesia, ramage genealogies and narratives connected to them became fiercely competing 'histories' legitimating both peace settlements and conflict: start with Gilbert (1989: 83). In Melanesia, oral history memories of battles can be impressive enough, with seventeen major ones well remembered, for example, within the large Lani or Ilaga Dani complex (see Section 2.1) for the years *ca.* 1910–1977: Larson (1987: Append. A); and see above p. 37.

*tohunga* to ensure blood-spillers would not mingle with people before they were cleansed (Cowan 1930: 231–232).[43] Exiting and returning to the 'normal profane' (*noa*) after the sacredness war (as *tapu*) also involved the strange practice of 'biting the latrine' (the strong horizontal beam or *paepae* that braced places of excretion on cliff-tops) to express being at an edge between life and death (Hanson 1983: 77–81). And we learn of the practice of *taua muru* ('stripping party') from pioneer Anglican missionary Charles Baker (of the CMS or Christian Missionary Society) in the Bay of Islands (in 1840): this allowed an aggrieved party to devastate the fort settlement (*pâ*) of a serious offender's clan, removing all the canoes, weapons, clothes and stored food as they liked, as compensation (*utu*) or honourable recognition that wrong (a foolish killing, an attempt at witchcraft, an insult, serious theft etc.) had been done. This would work best between clans in the same tribe, we can infer, but would be likely to break up into war when two *hapuu* of different *iwi* would try it (Baker in Ballara 1976: 490–491).[44]

However, details in knowledge of Maori warfare come after it has been affected by modern weaponry, at a time when trade with foreigners was so intense for the securing of muskets for hunting and, more significantly, for intertribal war rather than for eliminating those foreigners looming as conquerors. The so-called inter-*iwi* Musket Wars, beginning as early as 1806 and dissipated by 1845, clearly surged when chiefly war-lord Hongi Hika (1772–1828) sought vengeance for the loss of his brothers and the war-leader in a northern intertribal battle at Moremonui Gully, after he realized more muskets were needed in war to allow for the time to reload. After trips to Australia, even England (to meet King George IV), Hongi Hika's arsenal steadily increased, partly because his missionary friend, CMS lay preacher Henry Kendall, 'went native' and (to the dismay of his superiors in Sydney) started trading in muskets (Vayda 1974: 580–584; Crosby 2014; Ballara 2003: 393–443 et passim). The eventual flow-on effect in a southward movement of military expeditions was devastating, because tribes had long histories

---

[43] Manslayer 'cleansing' having some parallels in Melanesia: for example, Williams (1930: 173–175).

[44] Note Mead (2003: 186–187) on land given to allies in compensation after war.

of antipathy and could not wait to settle scores with superior weaponry. In an arms race that involved around 3,000 battles, extending attacks to unsuspecting tribes in the South Island meant the serious decimation of Maori populations and near genocide for the peace-preferring Moriori on the Chatham Islands (McLintock 1949: 36–40, 48–51; 78–96; King 2017: 28–59).[45]

It is fair enough to conclude that Micronesian and Polynesian conflict was affected by geographical smallness of scale and that tribes jostled for limited resources, including land. Still, feuding over killings, chiefly grudges over significant family deaths fuelling them, is the main theme of oral-historical accounts and traditional perceptions: overwhelmingly, 'blood is their argument' (cf. Meggitt 1977), while particular pretexts gave excuse for prolonging enmities. Aotearoa was exceptionally large, and land does not become the issue until later (in the land wars against the foreigners), just as in Melanesia's New Guinea Highlands land was less of an issue until the modern-medical curing of diseases (such as yaws), which resulted in the fastest-growing population on earth in the 1960s and 1970s (Trompf 1998: 216; Harris 1976).[46] Intriguingly and perhaps paradoxically, odd cases of attempted extermination are stronger in Polynesia than Melanesia, with the Moriori example, the annihilation of the isolated Eïao islanders by the Taipi 'man-eaters' of Nuku Hiva (Marquesas) in the 1800s, for another instance (Suggs 1962: 142), and some particularly vicious slaughtering by ambush on Samoa, with non-traditional weaponry rejected as inefficient (Bertholet 1879: 45). But overall, as also for Melanesia, let alone Micronesia, the attribution of 'bloodthirstiness', certainly for its own sake, does not fairly pertain (see Sack 1976; Bieniek 2002: 29–39; with Layard 1942: 558 on psychological issues).

---

[45] On less early anxiety over the whites, start (cautiously) with Smith (1921: 143–144) (on the *Pakeha* as the pre-contact mythic white race of deities living on the Sea).

[46] For the biggest PNG highland complex, Meggitt (1977: 28–29, 330) questioningly stresses population pressure on land as a *traditional* cause of tribal war. Competition for land on small atolls is another matter – see Younger (2009).

2.3.2.2 Ethos

Our approach to wider Pacific Island warfare, for reasons shown en route, have been necessarily diachronic, and we can fairly take the same tack for other matters of violence, more because the longer contact with the outside world and its effects had time to 'take its toll' on savagery-associated custom. Just to direct the reader's attention to a variety of relevant matters, we can reflect back on some of the issues we covered for Melanesia. Outer Pacific Islanders grew up with stories of death and revenge – from Polynesia's north, with the Hawai'ian epic poem (*mele*) of Pele the volcano goddess falling in love with Lohiau, chief of Kauai, at a *Hula* festival, yet destroying him in her unpredictability, across to the far south, with the Moriori legend of the heroine Apakura, who 'would not put off' her purpose to avenge her son's death (Kalakaua 1888: 484–494). In the wider Pacific, beware that the ghosts of chiefs might work lethal unfinished business before moving on (Mageo and Howard 1996: 59, 130 etc.). Polynesians heard chants to raise the fighting spirit necessary for military action (as with Tahitian metaphors of 'whirlwind', 'north wind', 'rock-breaker', and 'rushing headlong like an angry boar!') and witnessed the carving of formidable ancestral figures at the entrances of their settlements (at the gates of the Maori *pâ* or fortified stockade most memorably), as well as the routine creative designing of weaponry, even the Moriori whalebone club bearing carefully carved serrations at the working edges and a carved bird's head for the handle (Alpers 1970: 171–193; Shand 1895: 38 and n. 20; cf. Moore 1997: 165–166). One of the most valuable old chiefly informants about pre-contact ways on Tikopia (the Polynesian outlier near the Solomons) felt his father had not lived a fulfilled life because he had not killed anyone for Taumako (the Red Eel deity), and for that reason he was said to have passed away too early (Firth 1959: 158). Commoners and enslaved captives bore the threat of heavy sanctions from the top, at least under less 'open' and more 'stratified' conditions. Theirs was the virtually feudal task of working the land (but not hunting), as on the Tongan group, yet they might be required for war at short notice, and even peacemaking between chiefs or warlords demanded at least one sacrificed human victim to clinch matters (Goldman 1955: 683–688; Williamson 1939: 44). On islands where original inhabitants had been conquered – the Lau group (eastern Fiji), for example, especially on the larger island of Taveuni and Vanua Balavu, being taken by Tonga – tilling villagers would have to flee into the mountains when Tongan chiefs fought it out for places to control (Grainger 1992: 30–31). When Maori warriors were in the thick of fighting, non-participants, women and children were expected to fast, for war was *tapu* (sacred as both action and occasion) ([Maning] 1884: 96, 114–117). Wherever a Maori warrior was known to have died, one would not pass without leaving a stick or object of acknowledgement (and not without concern for a ghost) (Cruise 1823: 186).

Thinking back on themes we pursued from Melanesian ethnologies and what we have said of Melanesian sanctions against tabu-breakers: in Micronesia and Polynesia they were not decided by elders in common but by recommendations to a chiefly apex and potentially more affected by personal decision, or perhaps some apparently trivial slighting, even if an accepted code of conduct or prohibiting (Haw. *kapu*) was in place (in Polynesia especially pertaining to behaviour before chiefs, gender relations, rules of food distribution and eating, as well as to violent actions), and chiefs (as among the Maori) could deploy *makutu* ('sorcery sickness') as punishment (Hogbin 1934; cf. Bainbridge 2016). In intra-tribal quarrels or between close patrilineages, lethal weaponry was avoided and personal combat-wrestling preferred, although fathers on Rarotonga might expect their sons to oust them in a wrestling struggle (*kukumi anga*) that then left them despoliated and without further social influence (Williams 1837: 36). Reflecting also on sorcery, on balance in wider Oceania it was used more for group protection in priestly circles than for the lethal manoeuvres found in Melanesia, but sudden allegations of its inimical deployment certainly provided one trigger for war among the Maori (i.e., *makutu* as either sorcery or witchcraft) (Ballara 1976: 491).

Regarding Micronesian and Polynesian gender relations, the typical ascription of 'traditional roles and responsibilities' between men and women was accepted as 'divinely sanctioned and unchallenged', but with women having less chance of making a 'great name' and more chance of facing violence if they disturbed the systems (Tongamoa 1988: 89). Exclusion of females from sacred places was the norm (Williams 1837: 138–139; Burrows 1939; Lee 1992: 193–199). Yet royals and well-connected women gained special advantages. Punishments befell Samoan men of higher status for not recognizing the role of *feagaiga*, the sacred covenant to protect their sisters, who had potential to be priestesses, healers and peace negotiators (Fairbairn-Dunlop 1998), though women would have to join in (as on Upolu) when it was their family's turn to plead for the deified lady Taisumalie to bring health, fertility and victory, to bash and bleed heads in ascetic devotions (Turner 1884: 56–57). On the Marquesas Islands, women priests dominated in cult life, and warriors expressed their envy over the female power to give birth by undergoing top-to-bottom tattoos, so that they, too, might bring into being another body (Gell 1995). In child-rearing practice across the wider Pacific, a rather high rate of infanticide was reported; and the high degree of sacrificial slaughter – including documented savage attacks on animals or accounts of the trees and gardens of enemies meeting requital – cannot pass unnoticed (though Micronesians and Polynesians, on balance, seemed less ready to tamper with other peoples' cultic *sacra*).[47]

Of serious scribblings about such matters in so complex and vast an ethnological scene there is no end! But having faced the intense variegation of violent behaviour in traditional Pacific life-ways, made all the more difficult to handle because historical research into old records needs combining with anthropological know-how, another companion Element needs to follow to explain further what happens to the old religions under the impact of massive social change and modernization.

## 3 Afterthoughts and Foreshadowings

It has not been easy to write an Element on ostensibly depressing and negative aspects of cultures spanning across a third of the Earth's surface, but I have taken this Series to require a fixed concentration on the harm-dealing side of

---

[47] On questions of infanticide for apparently different reasons: for exampe, to encourage sons against daughters among Tahitian nobles (*areoi*), Tahiti (Tyerman and Bennet, 1831: vol. 1, 53, 196, 326); or as infant war victims, killed by young children to initiate them into slaughter (Ellis, 1842: vol. 3, p. 341); or in times of famine (Hawai'i) (Tobbin 1997: 68) etc. See also Best (1942: 248) (Maori destroying enemies' trees); compare Stürzenhofecker (1998: 57–58) (on NG Southern Highland Duna smashing 'all but one' of an enemy group's sacred stones).

human behaviour, treated dispassionately, with judicious examples and a fair-minded accounting of highly diverse insular circumstances. Readers should appreciate, given my other works which better balance matters out, that the Pacific can still live up to its name and that the 'dark anthropology' of unwelcome injuriousness need not oust 'the anthropology of the good' (Robbins 2013; Ortner 2016). Yet how painful it has been to suppress attention to the positive and non-violent! – all the astounding ritualized deeds of hospitality, the excited gift-giving and exchanges, rejoicings, self-decorating, comic pastiche, artistic expression of the ancestors, cooperative architecture, cunning inventions, garden spells and love magic, the youthful joking, girlish tittering and children's collective laughter in village life, together with distinctively religious concepts, symbols, precepts, codes of propriety, and rites that can be considered aside from actualizations of brute force. And just ponder the strict asceticism and sky-knowledge of those guiding and bearing the ordeal of a long-distant voyage!

Without deviating from our agenda, though, this Element raises certain dialectical questions about violence and religion, impelling us to ask whether 'religion' and 'violence' depend on each other. Considering such concern the Pacific Islander warrior or martial societies have shown to achieving both prowess and security, the answer obviously has to be in the affirmative. To compose some high-level theoretical formulation of this interdependence is tempting – that, for the human psyche, life depends on ('sacrificial') killing, for example, or that solidarity demands 'scapegoating the other' (Girard 1972; 1989) – but will be too sorely tested by exceptions and peculiarities in the Pacific diversity (Trompf 2004h). Generally for Oceania, though, the neighbouring groups at war and/or in exchange relations hold in common the same mental dictionaries and conceptual interests, whether to shout insults at each other or make workable arrangements, or share enough of their 'assumptive worlds' expressed as intelligible counterpoint to reinforce both sides. As a working agenda of orientation, serious matters for careful assessment lie in the reckonings and dialectical processes that go on as each perceived set of events and its outcomes unfold. In the transactions of trade or give-and-take, we expect both 'sides' to benefit 'positively' in some way, unless the patent inequality of an exchange amounts to an insult. When a death occurs, by comparison, in the dialectic of affairs we expect a killing, open or surreptitious, to be sheer negation. But of course it never is quite like this. Clearly, for the directly aggrieved, it is utterly wrenching and the reason for further negativity once the source of the death is 'established' (often involving specialists' divination). On the other hand, someone from either side might benefit in a recognizable typed way, and, while the enemy might glory in a small victory, the victim's widow will expect 'death payments' in due course, maybe even release from a difficult husband; or, if the dead man died fighting for allies, his clan can expect to be compensated. In each case, the intricacies need to be thought through; and if, above all, this will be the ongoing task of those 'in the thick of it', a thorough outside researcher ought to 'get the hang of it'.

There are always conundrums to face, especially relativities from both the indigenous viewpoint and an outsider's perspective. In every society, shared values will always be put to the test: in traditional situations, the priority of survival is likely to be decisive, but leaders (or rulers, as in high-chiefdoms) can act by whim against counsellors' expectancies. Who can best apprize leaders' decisions about the uses of violence, and on what basis? We have already discovered that avenging the enemy in traditional Pacific societies can be rewarded as a mark of prowess: is it not reasonable to adjudge a warrior like a soldier defending a nation, however small (Faidiban 2012: 74)? An outsider might be tempted to pre-judge violent acts in so-called tribal societies by universalist principles. Would not all mutilation, including on oneself, be against general standards for bodily care, including the periodic gashing of the penis by Wogeo males, a time-honoured practice to copy menstruation (Hogbin 1970: 88–91), or skin-cutting as an initiatory trial for young women among the Negrie (Camp 1979: 75)? Would not all cannibalism be violent, let us ask, as a fair rule? But for the Fore (PNG Eastern Highlands), to consume your loved ones, even while accepting they might have died through sorcery, is an act of sad respect, not a violation nor a buoyant 'feasting on my enemy' (Lindenbaum 1979;[48] cf. Stewart and Strathern 1999). And the allusion to sorcery will also

---

[48] The rare *kuru* (shaking) disease among the Fore gets incurred through women and children eating the brains of the dead, such endocannibalism being said to free the deceased's spirit.

draw to mind that there remain competing judgements about it, as to whether it is a useful inhibiter of inequalities that have come with entry into the modern economy – though many defenders of it today might draw a line somewhere and condemn assault sorcery or the plain use of poisons. Debates will go on.

Here parting issues beckon attention as to whether my own theoretical work on the logic of retribution (or 'payback logic') (Trompf esp. 1979: 92–106, 155–181, 1997; 2004a: 51–77; 2008a) gives explanatory direction to the ways religion and violence enmesh, and the question also presents itself as to the possibility of making practical recommendations about the *problématique* of religion and violence. Neither of these huge matters of enquiry can be satisfactorily handled unless we take our investigations further, to assess what happens to islanders' customary life-ways under the pressures of very serious interventions from the outside world and massive social change. Old ways come under threats and impositions of pacification, enforced by colonial and then national edicts. If violence was so integral to tradition, do the old spirit beings and former patterns of aggression pass away with each other? A great authority on the Maori, Te Rangi Hiroa, once asseverated that once the *tohunga* (priestly specialists) went 'out of business', the gods and their *mana* went with them, divinities being dependent on human mediums for their effect, even their life (Hiroa/Buck 1950: 519). But do religions and violence have such simple demises? We must await a subsequent companion Element to find out – to see what happens to Pacific Islander religiosities in their resilience and metamorphoses and how exertions of violent action take on more varied forms; and then to assess the emergent social problems demanding attention in the contemporary Pacific.

# References

Adams, H. (comp.). 1901. *Tahiti: Memoirs of Arii Taimai E. Marama of Eimeo Terirere*. Paris.

Aerts, T. 1998. *Traditional Religion in Melanesia*. Port Moresby.

Ahrens, T. 1986. *Unterwegs nach der verlorenen Heimat*. Erlangen.

Alaima Talu, A., et al. 1979. *Kiribati* (eds H. van Trease et al.). Tarawa.

Allen, M. 1967. *Male Cults and Secret Initiations in Melanesia*. Melbourne.

Alpers, A. (coll.) 1970. *Legends of the South Sea*. London.

Anati, E. 2020. *The Origins of Religion*. Brescia.

Anderson, A., K. Green, and F. Leach (eds). 2009. *Vastly Ingenious*. Dunedin.

Avosa, M. Forthcoming. *Moripi Landmarks*, Sydney.

Baal, J. van. 1966. *Dema: Description and Analysis of Marind-Anim Culture*. The Hague.

Babadzan, A. 1993. *Des Dépouilles des dieux: Essai sur la religion tahitienne*. Paris.

Ballara, A. 1976. 'The Role of Warfare in Maori Society in the Early Contact Period'. *Journal of the Polynesian Society* 85, 4: 487–506.

2003. *Taua: "Musket Wars," "Land Wars" or Tikanga?* Auckland.

Bambridge, T. (ed.). 2016. *The Rahui: Legal Pluralism in Polynesian Traditional Management*. Canberra.

Barker, J. (ed.). 2007. *The Anthropology of Morality in Melanesia*. Aldershot.

Barrow, J. (1831) 1980. *The Mutiny of the Bounty* (ed. G. Kennedy). Boston.

Barth, F. 1975. *Ritual and Knowledge among the Baktaman*. Oslo.

Bartle, N. 2005. *Death, Witchcraft and the Spirit World in the Highlands of Papua New Guinea*. Goroka.

Bateson, G. 1958. *Naven*. Stanford.

Bellwood, P. 1978. *Man's Conquest of the Pacific*. London.

Benedict, R. 1935. *Patterns of Culture*. London.

Bennett, J. 1974. 'Cross-Cultural Influences on Village Relocation on the Weather Coast of Guadalcanal, Solomon Islands, c. 1870–1953'. Master's dissertation, University of Hawai'i, Honolulu.

Berndt, R. M. 1962. *Excess and Constraint*. Chicago.

1964. 'Warfare in the New Guinea Highlands'. *American Anthropologist* (special issue) 66: 183–203.

Bernice P. Bishop Museum. 1892. *A Preliminary Catalogue of the Bernice Pauahi Bishop Museum of Polynesian Ethnology*. Part II. Honolulu.

Bertholet, S. 1879. *Journal d'un voyageur*. Paris.

Best, E. 1924. 'The Polynesian Method of Generating Fire'. *Journal of the Polynesian Society* 33: 87–102.

1942 *Forest Lore of the Maori*. Wellington.

Bielo, J. S. 2015. *The Anthropology of Religion*. Abingdon.

Bieniek, J. 2002. 'Enga and Evangelisation'. Doctoral dissertation, University of Sydney, Sydney.

Biersack, A. 1995. 'Introduction: The Huli, Duna, and Ipili Peoples Yesterday and Today'. In *Papuan Borderlands* (ed. A. Biersack), pp. 1–54. Ann Arbor, MI.

Binney, J. (ed.). 2007. *Te Kerikeri 1770–1850*. Nelson.

Bodrogi, T. 1967. 'Malangans of North New Ireland: L. Bíró's Unpublished Notes'. *Acta Ethnographica Acadamiae Scientarum Hungaricae* 16, 1–2: 63–77.

Bott, E. 1982. *Tongan Society at the Time of Captain Cook's Visits*. Wellington.

Brennan, P. W. 1977. *Let Sleeping Snakes Lie*. Adelaide.

Brumbauge, R. 1987. 'The Rainbow Serpent on the Upper Sepik'. *Anthropos* 82, 1/3: 25–32.

Brunton, R. 1980. 'Misconstrued Order in Melanesian Religion'. *Man* NS 15, 1: 112–128.

Brutti, L. 1997. 'Waiting for God: Ecocosmological Transformations among the Oksapmin'. In *Millennial Markers* (eds. P. Stewart and A. Strathern), pp. 87–131. Townsville.

Bulmer, R. 1965. 'The Kyaka of the Western Highlands'. In *Gods, Ghosts and Men in Melanesia* (eds. P. Lawrence and M. J. Meggitt ), pp. 132–167. Melbourne.

1968. 'Strategies of Hunting in New Guinea'. *Oceania* 38, 4: 302–308.

Bulmer, R. and S. 1962. 'Figurines and Other Stones of Power among the Kyaka of Central New Guinea'. *Journal of the Polynesian Society* 71, 2: 192–208.

Burridge, K. O. L. 1965. 'Tangu, Northern Madang District'. In *Gods, Ghosts and Men in Melanesia* (eds. P. Lawrence and M. J. Meggitt), pp. 224–249. Melbourne.

1975. 'The Melanesian Manager'. In *Studies in Social Anthropology* (eds. J. H. Beattie and R. G. Lienhardt), pp. 86–104. Oxford.

Burrows, E. G. 1939. 'Breed and Border in Polynesia'. *Journal of the Polynesian Society* 41, 1: 1–21.

Burton-Bradley, B. G. 1976. *Stone-Age Crisis*. Nashville.

Cain, H. 1979. *Aitu*. Wiesbaden.

Camp, C. 1979. 'A Female Initiatory Rite in the Neigrie Area'. In *Powers, Plumes and Piglets* (ed. N. Habel), pp. 68–83. Adelaide.

Campbell, J. C. 1980. 'The Historiography of Charles Savage'. *Journal of the Polynesian Society* 89, 2: 143–166.

Cassanti, J. L., and J. Hickman. 2014. 'New Directions in the Anthropology of Morality'. *Anthropological Theory* 14, 3: 252–262.

Chalmers, J., and W. Gill. 1885. *Work and Adventure in New Guinea*. London.

Chapman, P. M., and G. W. Gill. 1997. 'An Analysis of Easter Island Population History'. In *Easter Island in Pacific Context* (eds. C. M. Stevenson, G. Lee and F. J. Morin), pp. 143–150. Los Osos, CA.

Chinnery, E. P. 1919. 'The Application of Anthropological Methods to Tribal Development in New Guinea'. *Journal of the Royal Anthropological Institute* 49: 36–41.

Chowning, A. 1975. 'Lakalai Religion and World View and the Concept of "Seaboard Religion"'. In *Melanesian and Judaeo-Christian Religious Traditions* (ed. G. W. Trompf ), Bk. 1, pp. 75–104. Port Moresby.

Clarke, W. C. 1973. 'Temporary Madness as Theatre: Wildman Behaviour in New Guinea'. *Oceania* 43, 3: 198–214.

Clunie, F. 1977. *Fijian Weapons and Warfare*. Suva.
   2013. '*Tapua*: Polished "Ivory Shrines" of Tongan Gods'. *Journal of the Polynesian Society* 122, 1: 161–210.

Cochrane, E. E., and T. L. Hunt (eds.). 2018. *The Oxford Handbook of Prehistoric Oceania*. Oxford.

Codrington, R. H. 1891. *The Melanesians*. Oxford.

Coella de la Rosa, A. 2015. *Jesuits at the Margins*. New York.

Collingwood, R. G. 1939. *Essay on Metaphysics*. Oxford.

Collins, R. 2008. *Violence: A Micro-Sociological Theory*. Princeton.

Cook, J. 1821. *The Three Voyages Round the World*, vols 1, 3. London.
   1961 *Journals* (ed. J. C. Beaglehole), 5 vols. Cambridge.

Cowan, J. 1930. *The Maori Yesterday and To-day*. Auckland.

Cowan, J., and P. D. Hasselberg. (1922) 1983. *The New Zealand Wars*, vol. 2. Wellington.

Cox, M. P, 2013. 'Southeast Asian Islands and Oceania'. In *Encyclopedia of Human Migration* (eds. I. Ness and P. Bellwood), vol. 1, ch. 37. Oxford.

Crawley, E. 1934. *Oath, Curse and Blessing* (ed. T. Besterman). London.

Crook, P. 2003. *Darwinism, War and History*. Cambridge.

Crosby, R. D. 2014. *The Musket Wars*. Sydney.

Cruise, R. A. 1823. *Journal of a Ten Months' Residence in New Zealand*. London.

Cummins, H. G. 1977. 'Tongan Society at the Time of European Contact'. In *Friendly Islands* (ed. N. Rutherford ), pp. 63–89. Melbourne.

Cunningham, L. J. 1992. *Ancient Chamorro Society*. Honolulu.

D'Arcy, P. 2018. *Transforming Hawai'i*. Canberra.

Dalton, D. 2007. 'When Is It Moral To Be a Sorcerer?' In *The Anthropology of Morality in Melanesia* (ed. J. Barker), pp. 39–55. Aldershot.

Dark, P. J. C. 1974. *Kilenge Life and Art: A Look at a New Guinea People*. London.

Daugherty, J. S. 1979. 'Polynesian Warfare and Fortifications'. Master's dissertation, University of Auckland, Auckland.

Deacon, A. B. 1934. *Malekula* (ed. C. H. Wedgwood). London.

Déniau, A. 1901. 'Croyances religieuses et mœurs des indigènes de l'île Malo'. *Les Missions Catholiques* 23: 346–359.

Dennen, J. van der, and V. Falger (eds.). 1990. *Socio-Biology and Conflict*. London.

Diamond, J. 2005. *Collapse*. Melbourne.

    2013 *The World until Yesterday*. Melbourne.

Dinnen, S., and A. Ley (eds.). 2013. *Reflections on Violence in Melanesia*. Canberra.

Dittner, W. (coll.). 1907. *Te Tohunga*. London.

Driessen, H. 2005. 'Tupai'a: The Trials and Tribulations of a Polynesian Priest'. In *Vision and Reality in Pacific Religion* (eds. P. Herda, M. Reilly and D. Hilliard), ch. 4. Canberra.

Dubois, M. J. 1970. 'Les Grands refuges de guerre de Nnaened à Maré, Nouvelle-Calédonie'. *Journal de la Société des Océanistes* 26: 55–60.

Dupeyrat, A. 1955. *Festive Papua* (trans. E. de Mauney). London.

    1964. *Briseurs de lances chez les Papous*. Paris.

Dyson, J. [part auth.]. 1996. *Among the Islands of the Pacific* (abridg. C. Rundell). Sydney.

Earle, T. 1997. *How Chiefs Come to Power*. Stanford.

Eastburn, D. 1976. 'The Mendi'. Unpublished book in typescript, Mendi High School, Mendi.

Eibl-Eibesfelt, I. 1991. *Krieg und Frieden aus der Sicht der Verhaltensforschung*. Munich.

Ellis, W. 1842. *Polynesian Researches*, vols 3–4. London.

Epstein, A. L. 1984. *The Experience of Shame in Melanesia*. London.

Eri, V. 1970. *The Crocodile*. Harmondsworth.

Eskridge, R. L. 1931. *Manga Reva*. Indianapolis.

Faidiban, D. 2012. 'Accused of Being a Separatist'. In *Governing New Guinea* (ed. L. Visser), pp. 55–80. Leiden.

Fairbairn-Dunlop, P. 1998. *Tamaitai Samoa*. Carson, CA.

Farrer, D. S., and J. D. Sellmann. 2016. 'Chants of Re-enchantment'. In *War Magic* (ed. D. S. Farrer), pp. 133–140. New York.

Fastré, P. 1937. 'Moeurs et coutoumes Fouyougheses'. Unpublished typescript, Sacred Heart Mission, Popole, PNG.

Feil, D. 1987. *The Evolution of Highland Papua New Guinea Societies*. Cambridge.

Feinberg, R. 1988. 'Symbolic Structures and Social Space'. In *Beiträge zur Religion* (eds. G. Rinschede and K. Rudolph), pp. 11–27. Berlin.

Firth, R. 1957. *We the Tikopia*. London.

1959. 'Ritual Adzes in Tikopia'. In *Anthropology in the South Seas* (eds. J. D. Freeman and W. R. Geddes), pp. 149–156. New Plymouth.

Fison, L. 1884. 'The Nanga or Sacred Stone Enclosure of Wainimala'. *Journal of the Royal Anthropological Institute* 14: 13–31.

Fitzpatrick, S. M., and G. C. Nelson. 2008. 'From Limestone Caves to Concrete Graves: 3000 Years of Mortuary Practice in the Palau Archipelago'. *International Journal of Osteoarchaeology* 18, 5: 439–457.

Foin, T. C., and W. G. Davis. 1984. 'Ritual and Self-Regulation of the Tsembaga Maring Ecosystem'. *Human Ecology* 12, 4: 385–412.

Forge, A. 1970. 'Prestige, Influence and Sorcery'. In *Witchcraft Confessions and Accusations* (ed. M. Douglas), pp. 257–275. London.

Fortune, R. (1932) 1963. *Sorcerers of Dobu*. New York.

Fox, C. E., and F. H. Drew. 1915. 'Beliefs and Tales of San Cristoval'. *Journal of the Royal Anthropological Institute* 45: 131–185.

Garanger, J. 1982. *Archaeology of the New Hebrides* (trans. R. Groube). Sydney.

García, F. (1683) 2004. *The Life and Martyrdom of the Venerable Father Diego Luis de San Vitores* (trans. and ed. J. A. McDonough). Mangilao.

Gardner, R., and K. Heider. 1969. *Gardens of War*. New York.

Gell, A. 1995. 'Closure and Multiplication'. In *Cosmos and Society in Oceania* (eds D. de Coppet and A. Iteanu), pp. 43–54. Oxford.

Germer, E. (dir.). 1965. *Waffen de Südsevölker*. Leipzig.

Gesch, P. 2001. 'On Conversion from the Global to the Local'. In *The End of Religions?* (eds. C. M. Cusack and P. Oldmeadow), pp. 1–10. Sydney.

'Talking *Sanguma*'. 2015. In *Talking it Through* (eds. M. Forsyth and R. Eves), ch. 6. Canberra.

Gewertz, D. 1983. *Sepik River Societies*. New Haven.

Gibbs, P. (ed.). 2003. *Attitudes and Practice towards Persons with Disabilities*. Goroka.

Gibbs, P., and J. J. Wailoni. 2009. 'Sorcery and a Christian Response in the East Sepik'. In *Sanguma in Paradise* (ed. F. Zocca), pp. 55–96. Goroka.

Gifford, E. W. 1929. *Tongan Society*. Honolulu.

Gilbert, A. F. 1989. *Tungaru Traditions*. Honolulu.

Gillison, G. 1993. *Between Culture and Fantasy*. Chicago.

Girard, R. N. T. 1972. *Violence and the Sacred* (trans. P. Gregory). Baltimore.

1989. *The Scapegoat* (trans. Y. Freccero). Baltimore.

Glasse, R. M. 1965. 'The Huli of the Southern Highlands'. On *Gods, Ghosts and Men in Melanesia* (eds. P. Lawrence and M.J. Meggitt), pp. 27–49. Melbourne.

Glasse, R.M. 1968. *The Huli*. Paris.

Glick, L. B., 1973. 'Sorcery and Witchcraft'. In *Anthropology in Papua New Guinea* (ed. I. Hogbin), pp. 182–185. Melbourne.

Godelier, M., and M. Strathern (eds.). 1991. *Great Men and Big Men*. Cambridge.

Goldman, I. 1955. 'Status Rivalry and Cultural Evolution in Polynesia'. *American Anthropologist* 57: 680–697.

1970. *Ancient Polynesian Society*. Chicago.

Golson, J. 1959. 'Culture Change in Prehistoric New Zealand'. In *Anthropology in the South Seas* (eds. J. D. Freeman and W. R. Geddes), pp. 29–74. New Plymouth.

1981. 'Agriculture in New Guinea: The Long View'. In *A Time to Plant and a Time to Uproot* (eds. D. Denoon and C. Snowdon), pp. 33–41. Port Moresby.

2008. 'The Ipomoean Revolution Revisited: Society and the Sweet Potato in the Upper Wahgi Valley'. In *Peoples of the Pacific* (ed. P. D'Arcy), pp. 119–154. New York.

Golson, J., et al. (eds.). 2017. *Ten Thousand Years of Cultivation at Kuk Swamp*. Canberra.

Grainger, G. 1992. *Wainiqolo: Last Polynesian Warlord*. Sydney.

Green, R. 1967. 'The Immediate Origins of the Polynesians'. In *Polynesian Culture History*, pp. 215–240. Honolulu.

1970. *Review of the Prehistoric Sequence in the Auckland Province*. Dunedin.

Grey, Sir G. (1855) 1929. *Polynesian Mythology*. Auckland.

Grijp, P. van der. 2014. *Manifestations of Mana*. Berlin.

*References*

Gunson, N. 1962. 'An Account of the Mamaia or Visionary Heresy of Tahiti, 1826–1841'. *Journal of the Polynesian Society* 71, 2: 208–245.

1969. 'Pomare II of Tahiti and Polynesian Imperialism'. *Journal Pacific History* 4: 65–82.

1987. 'Sacred Female Chiefs and Female "Headmen" in Polynesian History'. *Journal of Pacific History* 22, 3: 138–172.

Hage, P., and F. Harary. 1996. *Island Networks*. Cambridge.

Hallpike, C. 1977. *Bloodshed and Vengeance in the Papuan Mountains*. Oxford.

Hanson, F. A., and L. 1983. *Counterpoint in Maori Culture*. London.

Harris, G. T. 1976. 'Some Responses to Population Pressure in the Papua New Guinea Highlands'. *UPNG Economics Department Discussion Paper* (Sept.): 1–29.

Heine-Geldern, R. 1932. 'Urheimat und früheste Wanderungen der Austronesier'. *Anthropos* 27, 3–4: 543–619.

Henry, T. 1928. *Ancient Tahiti*. Honolulu.

Herdt, G. H. (ed.). 1993. *Ritualized Homosexuality in Melanesia*. Berkeley.

Heyerdahl, T. 1952. *American Indians in The Pacific*. London.

Heyerdahl, T., and E. N. Ferdon. 1961. 'Addendum'. In *Reports of the Norwegian Archaeological Expedition to Easter Island* (eds. T. Heyerdahl and E. N. Ferdon), vol. 2, pp. 325–327. New York.

Hezel, F. 1983. *The First Taint of Civilization*. Honolulu.

2015. *When Cultures Clash*. Garapan.

Hezel, F., and J. Dobbin. 2011. *Summoning the Powers Beyond*. Honolulu.

Hickman, J. 2014. 'Ancestral Personhood and Moral Justification'. *Anthropological Theory* 14, 3: 317–335.

Hiltbrand, R. (ed.). 1962. *Verarbeitung und Verwendung von Stein und Muschelschalen*. Berlin.

Hiroa, T.R./Buck, P. 1932. *Ethnology of Tongareva*. Honolulu.

1934. *Mangaian Society*. Honolulu.

1936. *Regional Diversity and the Elaboration of Sorcery in Polynesia*. New Haven.

1950. *The Coming of the Maori*. Wellington.

Hirsch, E. 2008. 'Knowing, not Knowing, Knowing Anew'. In *Knowing how to Know* (eds. N. Hapstead, E. Hirsch, and J. Okely), pp. 21–37. Oxford.

Hocart, A. M. 1927. *Kingship*. London.

Hogbin, I. 1934. *Law and Order in Polynesia*. London.

1964. *A Guadalcanal Society*. New York.

1970. *The Island of Menstruating Men*. London.

1978. *Leaders and the Led*. Melbourne.

Hommon, R. J. 2016. *The Ancient Hawai'ian Origins*. Oxford.

Huber, M. T. 1987. 'Constituting the Church: Catholic Missionaries on the Sepik Frontier'. *American Ethnologist* 14, 1: 107–125.

Huffman, K. 2019. '"Blad i mas ron": "Blood must Flow": Pigs, Souls, Sacrifice, Status and Eternity in Northern Vanuatu'. *Arts & Cultures* (Geneva) 20 (April): 200–17.

Hughes, P. 1977. 'The Use of Resources in Traditional Melanesia'. In *The Melanesian Environment* (ed. J. H. Winslow), pp. 28–34. Canberra.

Ionesov, V. I., and G. W. Trompf (eds.). 2021. *Kultura kak Mirotvorchestvo*. Samara.

Iteanu, A. 1990. 'The Concept of the Person and the Ritual System'. *Man* NS 25, 1: 35–53.

Ivens, W. G. 1930. *Island Builders of the Pacific*. London.

Jedin, H. 1971 *Handbuch der Kirchengeschichte*, vol. 2. Freiburg im Breisgau.

Jenkins, C., et al. 1989. 'Culture Change and Epidemiological Patterns among the Hagahai'. *Human Ecology* 17, 1: 27–55.

Jensen, A. E. 1951. *Mythos und Kult bei Naturvölkern*. Wiesbaden.

Jessep, O. 1974. 'Land Tenure in Barok, New Guinea'. Doctoral dissertation, Australian National University, Canberra.

Jochim, M. A. 1981. *Strategies for Survival*. New York.

Kalakaua, Kg. D. 1888. *The Legends and Myths of Hawaii*. New York.

Kamakau, S. M. 1991. *Ka Poʻe Kahiko* (trans. M. K. Pukui, ed. D. B. Barrère). Honolulu.

Kamma, F. C. (ed.). 1975. *Religious Texts of the Oral Traditions from Western New Guinea*. Leiden.

1981. *Ajaib di Mara Kita*, vol. 1. Jakarta.

Keeley, L. H. 1996. *War before Civilization*. Oxford.

Keesing, R. M. 1975. *Kin Groups and Social Structure*. New York.

1982. *Kwaio Religion*. New York.

Kelly, R. C. 1976. 'Witchcraft and Sexual Relations'. In *Man and Woman in the New Guinea Highlands* (eds. P. Brown and G. Buchbinder), pp. 33–53. Washington DC.

1993. *Constructing Inequality*. Ann Arbor.

2000. *Warless Societies and the Origins of War*. Ann Arbor.

Ketobwau, I. T. 1994. 'Tuma – the Trobriand Heaven'. Bach. Div. dissertation, Rarongo Theological College, Rabaul.

King, D. S. 2011 *Food for the Flames*. San Francisco.

King, M. 2017 *Moriori*. Wellington.

Kirch, P. V. 2010. 'Peopling of the Pacific'. *Annual Review of Anthropology* 39: 131–146.

2017. *On the Road of the Winds*. Berkeley.

Knauft, B. M. 1976. *Good Company and Violence*. Berkeley.

1985. 'Melanesian Warfare'. *Oceania* 60, 4: 250–311.

1999. *From Primitive to Postcolonial in Melanesia*. Ann Arbor.

Kolb, M. J., and B. Dixon. 2002. 'Landscapes of War'. *American Antiquity* 667, 3: 514–534.

Krämer, A. 1902–1903. *Die Samoa Inseln I–II*, 2 vols. Stuttgart.

Kuehling, S. 2005 *Dobu*. Honolulu.

2014. 'The Converted War Canoe'. *Anthropologica* 56, 2: 269–284.

Kuschel, R., 1998. *Vengeance is their Reply*, 2 vols. Copenhagen.

Kyakas, A., and P. W. Wiessner. 1992. *From Inside the Women's House*. Brisbane.

Lacey, R. 1973. 'Some Thoughts from a Wandering Historian'. *Catalyst* 3, 2: 37–47.

1985. '*To Limbimbur*, the "Wanderers"'. *Pacific Studies* 9, 1: 98–99.

Lambert, S. M. 1934, *The Depopulation of Pacific Races*. Honolulu.

Larson, G. 1987. 'The Structure and Function of the Cycle of Warfare among the Ilaga Dani'. Doctoral dissertation, University of Michigan, Ann Arbor.

Lasaulx, E. von. 1854. *Philosophie der Geschichte*. Munich.

Lawrence, P. 1984. *The Garia*. Melbourne.

1987. '*De Rerum natura*'. In *Sorcerer and Witch in Melanesia* (ed. M. Stephen), pp. 17–40. Melbourne.

Layard, J. 1942. *Stone Men of Malekula*. London.

Lee, B. X. 2019. *Violence*. Oxford.

Lee, G. 1992. *Rock Art of Easter Island*. Los Angeles.

Lessa, W. A. 1950. 'The Place of Ulithi in the Yap Empire'. *Human Organization* 9: 16–18.

Lindenbaum, S. 1979. *Kuru Sorcery*. Palo Alto, CA.

Linnekin, J. 1997. 'Contending Approaches'. In *Cambridge History of the Pacific Islanders* (eds, D. Denoon et al.), pp. 1–36. Cambridge.

Lockerby, W. (1809) 1925. *Journal, Sandalwood Trader*. London.

Loeb, E. M. 1978. *History and Traditions of Niue*. Honolulu.

Lohmann, R. I. (ed.). 2019. *Haunted Pacific*. Durham, NC.

Lornley, L., with D. Eastburn. 1976. 'The Mendi' (unpublished book in typescript, Mendi).

Luomala, K. 1951. *The* Menehune *of Polynesia*. Honolulu.

Lynch, J. D. 1998. *Pacific Languages*. Honolulu.

Mageo, J. M., and A. Howard (eds.). 1996. *Spirits in Culture*. New York.

Malinowski, B. 1920. 'War and Weapons among the Natives of the Trobriand Islands'. *Man* 20: 10–12.

    1926. *Crime and Custom in Savage Society*. London.

Malopa'upo, Isaia. 1999. *Coming of Age in American Anthropology*. New York.

[Maning, F.E. ] 1884. *Old New Zealand*. London.

Mantovani, E. (ed.) 1984. *An Introduction to Melanesian Religions*. Goroka.

Maretu. (1880) 1983. *Cannibals and Converts*. Suva.

Martin, J. (ed. [of W. Mariner]). (1818) 1827. *Account of the Natives of the Tonga Islands*, 2 vols. Edinburgh.

Marx, K. (1852) 1951. 'The Eighteenth Brumaire of Louis Bonaparte'. In K. Marx and F. Engels, *Selected Works* (English trans.), vol. 1, pp. 221–311. Moscow.

Maude, E. 1968. *Of Islands and Men*. Melbourne.

McLintock, A. H. 1949. *The History of Otago*. Dunedin.

Mead, H. M. 2003. *Tikanga Māori*. Wellington.

Mead, M. (1935) 1950. *Sex and Temperament in Three Primitive Societies*. New York.

Meggitt, M. J. 1977. *Blood Is Their Argument*. Brisbane.

Meier, J. 1913. 'Der Zauberei bei den Kustenbewohnern der Gazellehabinsel'. *Anthropos* 8: 1–11, 285–305, 688–713.

Merlan, F., and A. Rumsey. 1991. *Ku Waru: Language and Supplementary Politics*. Cambridge.

Mimica, J. 2007. 'Descended from the Celestial Rope'. In *Explorations in Psychoanalytic Ethnography* (ed. J. Mimica), pp. 77–105. Oxford.

Mitton, R. 1983. *The Lost World of Irian Jaya*. Oxford.

Mombi, G. F. 2019. 'Developing a Response to the Melanesian Concept of *Gutpela Sindaun*'. Doctoral dissertation, University of Otago, Dunedin, NZ.

Moore, A. 1997. *Arts in the Religions of the Pacific*. London.

Moorehead, A. 1966. *The Fatal Impact*. New York.

Moseley, M. E. 1975. *The Maritime Foundation of Andean Civilization*. Menlo Park.

Mosko, M. S. 2017. *Ways of Baloma*. London.

Moss, R. 1925. *Life and Death in Oceania*. London.

Muke, J. 1993. 'The Wahgi Opo Kumbo'. Doctoral dissertation, University of Cambridge, Cambridge.

Murray, G. 1928. *The Ordeal of this Generation*. London.

Murray, J. H. P. 1912. *Papua or British New Guinea*. London.

Narokobi, B. 1983. *The Melanesian Way*. Suva.

Newman, E. L. 1964. '"Wild Man" Behavior in a New Guinea Highland Community'. *American Anthropologist* 66: 1–19.

Nida, E. 1954. *Customs, Culture and Christianity*. London.

Numazawa, K. 1965. 'The Religion of the Kobon Tribe in Schrader Ranges'. *Journal of Religious Studies* (Tokyo) 39, 3, no. 186 (1965): 3–15.

O'Hanlon, M. 1989. *Reading the Skin*. London.

Oliver, D., 2002. *Polynesia in Early Historic Times*. Honolulu.
   2019 edn. *Ancient Tahitian Society*, 3 vols., online. Honolulu.

Oram, N. 1968. *Taurama*. Canberra.

Orbell, M. 1996. *Maori Myth and Legend*. Sydney.

Ortner, S. 2016. 'Dark Anthropology and its Others', *HAU* 6, 1: 47–73.

Otterbein, K. F. (ed.) 1994. *Feuding and Warfare*. Amsterdam.

Otto, T., H. Thrane, and K. Vandkilde (eds.). 2006. *Warfare and Society*. Aarhus.

Owsley, D. W., et al. 2016. 'Evidence for Injuries and Violent Death'. In *Skeletal Biology of the Ancient Rapanui* (eds. V. H. Stefan and G. W. Gill), pp. 222–252. Cambridge.

Oxenham, M., and H. Buckley (eds.). 2016. *Routledge Handbook of Bioarchaeology in Southeast Asia and the Pacific*. New York.

Parake, T. 1983. 'The Culture of the Kulaga Tribe'. Unpublished MS, Holy Spirit Seminary, Port Moresby.

Parratt, J. K. 1971. 'Papuan Marriage'. *Journal of the Papua and New Guinea Society* 5, 1: 3–14.

Patterson, M. 1974–1975. 'Sorcery and Witchcraft in Melanesia'. *Oceania* 45, 2: 132–160; 45, 3: 212–234.

Pech, R. 1991. *Manup and Kilibob*. Goroka.

Petersen, G. 2009. *Traditional Micronesian Societies*. Honolulu.

Pettifer, J., and R. Bradley. 1990. *Missionaries*. London.

Phear, S. 2007. *The Monumental Earthworks of Palau*. Oxford.

Phillips, C. 2001. *Waihou Journeys*. Auckland.

Ploeg, A. 1995. 'First Contact, in the Highlands of Irian Jaya'. *Journal of Pacific History* 30, 2: 227–239.

Poignant, A. and R., 1972. *Kaleku*. Sydney.

Pomare, Sir M., and J. Cowan. 1930. *Legends of the Maori*, 2 vols. Wellingtons.

Pospisil, L. 1958. *The Kapauka Papuans and their Law*. New Haven.

Rainbird, P. 2004. *The Archaeology of Micronesia*. Cambridge.

Ralph, R. (ed.). 2012. *The Archaeology of Violence*. Albany, NY.

Ramsay, E. 1975. *Middle Wahgi Dictionary*. Mount Hagen.

Ranger, T. 1992. 'The Invention of Tradition in Colonial Africa'. In *The Invention of Tradition* (eds. E. Hobsbawm and T. Ranger), ch. 6. Cambridge.

Rankine, J. et al. 2015. 'Pacific Peoples'. *Journal of Interpersonal Violence* 32, 18 (online: journals.sagepub.com).

Rappaport, R. A. 1967. 'Ritual Regulation of Environmental Relations among a New Guinea People'. *Ethnology* 6, 1: 17–30.

Read, K.E. 1966. *The High Valley*. New York.

Reay, M. 1974. 'Changing Conventions of Dispute Settlement in the Minj Area'. In *Contention and Dispute* (ed. A. L. Epstein), pp. 198–239. Canberra.

1987. 'The Magico-Religious Foundations of New Guinea Highlands Warfare'. In *Sorcerer and Witch in Melanesia* (ed. M. Stephen), pp. 83–120. Melbourne.

Reilly, M. 2001. 'Sex and War in Ancient Polynesia'. *Journal of the Polynesian Society* 110, 1: 31–57.

Rickard, R. 1891. 'The Dukduk Association of New Britain'. *Proceedings of the Royal Society of Victoria* N.S., 3: 70–76.

Rivers, W. H. R. 1914. *History of Melanesian Society*, vol. 2. Cambridge.
1922. *Essay on the Depopulation of Melanesia*. Cambridge.

Robarts, E. (1806) 1974. *The Marquesan Journal of Edward Roberts 1797–1824* (ed. G. Dening). Canberra.

Robbins, J. 2013. 'Beyond the Suffering Subject: Toward an Anthropology of the Good'. *Journal of the Royal Anthropological Institute* 19, 3: 447–462.

Rodman, M., and M. Cooper (eds.). 1983. *The Pacification of Melanesia*. Lanham.

Romilly, H. H. 1887. 'Memorandum'. *British New Guinea Annual Report 1887*, pp. 33–37. Brisbane.

Rossi, M. C. 2018. 'War Clubs as Art of the Western Islands, Manus'. In *Weapons, Culture and the Anthropology Museum* (eds. T. Crowley and A. Mills), pp. 119–132. Newcastle upon Tyne.

Rubel, P. G., and A. Rosman. 1978. *Your Own Pigs You May Not Eat*. Canberra.

Ryan, T. 2002. '"Le Président des Terres Australes": Charles de Brosses'. *Journal of Pacific History* 36, 2: 157–186.

Sack, P. 1976. *The Bloodthirsty Laewomba?* Lae.

Sahlins, M. 1958. *Social Stratification in Polynesia*. Seattle.
1963. 'Poor Man, Rich Man, Big Man, Chief'. *Comparative Studies in Society and History* 5: 285–303.
1983. 'Raw Women, Cooked Men, and Other "Great Things" of the Fiji Islands'. In *The Ethnography of Cannibalism* (eds. P. Brown and D. Tuzin), pp. 72–93. Washington.

Salzman, M. 1990. 'The Dynamics of Cultural Trauma'. In *Social Change and Psychosocial Adaptation in the Pacific Islands* (eds. A. J. Marsella, A. A. Austin and B. Grant ), pp. 29–51. New York.

Sand, C. 2000. 'Reconstructing "Traditional" Kanak Society in New Caledonia'. In *The Archaeology of Difference* (eds. R. Torrence and A. Clarke ), pp. 51–78. London.

Scarr, D. 2013. *A History of the Pacific Islands*. Richmond, UK.

Schieffelin, E. 1990. *The Sorrow of the Lonely and the Burning of the Dancers*. Brisbane.

Schmitz, C. A. 1962. 'Wildbeuter Problematik in Ozeanien'. *Paideuma* 8, 2: 124–135.

Schoeffel, P. 1987. 'Rank, Gender and Politics in Ancient Samoa'. *Journal of Pacific History* 22, 4: 174–194.

Schwimmer, E. 1973. *Exchange in the Social Structure of the Orokaiva*. Sydney.

Sears, S. V. 1998. 'Women Fighters in Polynesia'. Internet posting, www .stephaniesears.com.

Seligman, C. G. 1910. *The Melanesians of British New Guinea*. Cambridge.

Shand, A. 1895. 'The Moriori People of the Chatham Islands'. *Journal of the Polynesian Society* 4: 24–45.

Shaw, D. 1996. *From Longhouse to Village*. Orlando.

Shineberg, D. 1999. *The People Trade*. Honolulu.

Shutler, R. and M. E. 1975. *Oceanic Prehistory*. Menlo Park.

Siikala, J. 1992. *Cult and Conflict in Tropical Polynesia*. Helsinki.

Simmons, D. (trans. and ed.). 2003. *Ngâ Tau Rere*. Auckland.

Skoglund, P., et al. 2016. 'Geonomic Insights into the Peopling of the Southwest Pacific'. *Nature* 538, 7626: 510–513.

Smith, P. 1921. *Hawaiki*. Auckland.

Sokiveta, E. (part auth.) 1973. 'Indigenous Reporting: The Pig's Head (1854)'. In (and trans. by) A. R. Tippett, *Aspects of Pacific Ethnohistory*, pp. 91–104. Pasadena.

Spriggs, M. 1996. 'Chronology and Colonisation in Island Southeast Asia and the Pacific'. In *Oceanic Culture History* (eds. J. Davidson et al.), pp. 33–50. Dunedin.

Steinmetz, S. R. 1892–4. *Ethnologische Studien zur erster Entwicklung der Strafe*, 2 vols. Leipzig.

Stephen, M. 1980. 'Dream, Trance and Spirit Possession'. In *Religious Experience in World Religions* (ed. V.C. Hayes), pp. 25–49. Adelaide.

Stewart, P. J., and A. Strathern. 1999. 'Feasting on My Enemy'. *Ethnohistory* 46, 4: 545–569.

2002. *Violence: Theory and Ethnography*. London.

2003. 'The Ultimate Protest Statement: Suicide'. *Journal of Ritual Studies* 17, 1: 79–88.

2019. *Sacred Revenge in Oceania*. Cambridge.

Stewart, P. J., A. Strathern, I. Courtens and D. van Oosterhout (eds.). 2001. *Humors and Substances*. Westport, CN.

Stone-Wigg, M. J. 1909. 'The Papuans'. In *Mankind and the Church* (ed. H. H. Montgomery), pp. 3–69. London.

Strathern, A. 1968. 'Sickness and Frustration'. *Mankind* 6, 2: 545–551.

Strathern, A., and P. J. Stewart. 2011. 'Religion and Violence in Pacific Island Societies'. In *Violence and the World's Religious Traditions* (eds. M. Juergensmeyer, M. Kitts and M. Jerryson), ch. 8. Oxford.

2011. *Peace-Making and the Imagination*. Brisbane.

Stürzenhofecker, G. 1998. *Times Enmeshed*. Stanford.

Suggs, R. 1960. *The Island Civilization of Polynesia*. New York.

1962. *The Hidden Worlds of Polynesia*. New York.

Swain, T. 1993. *A Place for Strangers*. Cambridge.

Swain, T., and G. W. Trompf. 1995. *Religions of Oceania*. London.

Taumoefolau, J. 2012. *A Providence of War*. Sydney.

Ta'unga. (1846) 1968. *Works* (eds. R.G. and M. Crocombe). Canberra.

Tefft, S.K., and D. Reinhardt. 1974. 'Warfare Regulation'. *Behavior Science Research* 2: 151–172.

Temple, P. 2002. *The Last True* Explorer. Auckland.

Thayer, B. A. 2004. *Darwin and International Relations*. Lexington.

Thimme, H. M. 1977. 'Manarmakeri'. *Point* 1: 21–49.

Thomas, N. 1989. 'The Force of Ethnology: Origins and Significance of the Melanesia/Polynesia Distinction'. *Current Anthropology* 30, 1: 27–41.

   1990. *Marquesan Societies*. Oxford.

   1997. *In Oceania*. Durham, NC.

   2003. *Cook*. New York.

Thomson, P. 2008 *Kava in the Blood*. Charleston, NC.

Tobbin, J. 1997. 'Savages, the Poor, and the Discourse of Hawaiian Infanticide'. *Journal of the Polynesian Society* 106, 1: 65–92.

Tomasetti, F. 1976. *Traditionen und Christentum im Chimbu-Gebiet Neuguineas*. Wiesbaden.

Tongamoa, T. 1988. *Pacific Women*. Suva.

Toren, C. 1995. 'Cosmogonic Aspects of Desire and Compassion in Fiji'. In *Cosmos and Society in Oceania* (eds. D. de Coppet and A. Iteanu), pp. 57–82. Oxford.

Trompf, G. W. 1977. '"Ikaroa Raepa" of Keharo'. *Oral History* 5, 7: 32–42.

   1979. 'Man Facing Death and After-Life in Melanesia'. In P*owers, Plumes and Piglets* (ed. N. Habel), pp. 121–136. Adelaide.

   1979(–2022). *The Idea of Historical Recurrence in Western Thought*, 2 vols. Berkeley.

   1986 edn. 'Bilalaf'. In *Prophets of Melanesia* (ed. G.W. Trompf ), pp. 12–64. Suva.

   1988. 'Salvation in Primal Religion'. *Prudentia* (Suppl. No.) (Auckland), 207–231.

   1997. 'La logica della ritorsione'. *Religioni e Società* 12/28: 48–77.

1998. 'The Involvements of Religion in Population Planning'. In *Population and Global Security* (ed. N. Polunin), pp. 205–234. Cambridge.

2000. 'Melanesian and the Sacred'. In *Religion et sacré en Océanie* (ed. F. Angleviel), pp. 49–66. Paris.

2002. 'Easter Island: Site of the First Pacific Cargo Cult?' In *Ugo Bianchi* (ed. G. Casadio), pp. 441–465. Rome.

2004a edn. *Melanesian Religion*. Cambridge.

2004b. 'On Sacrificing Girard'. *Threskeiologia* (Athens) 5: 131–140.

2005 edn. *In Search of Origins*. Slough.

2006. *Religions of Melanesia*. Westport, CN.

2007. 'Ritualnye i identifikazionnye Markery v Melanezi: Etynohistoricheskye Pierspiektivy'. In *Socialnye innovacii v kulturnom procecce* (eds. A. V. Malafeev and V. Ionesov), pp. 146–169. Samara.

2008a. *Payback*. Cambridge.

2008b. 'Traditional Melanesian Religions'. In *Melanesian Religion and Christianity* (ed. G. W. Trompf ), pp. 8–59. Goroka.

2008c. 'Polynesia'. In *Encyclopedia of Religion and Nature* (eds. B. R. Taylor), vol. 2, pp. 1287–1288. New York.

2011. 'The Classification of the Sciences and the Quest for Interdisciplinarity'. *Environmental Conservation* 38, 2: 113–126.

(1964) 2012. 'Kon-Tiki and the Critics' (with retrospect). In *Written into History: Celebrating Fifty Years of the Melbourne Historical Journal 1961–2011* (eds. K. Wotherspoon and E. Rogers), pp. 81–101. Melbourne.

2012. 'Christianity in Melanesia'. In *Introducing World Christianity* (ed. C. Farhadian), pp. 244–258. Oxford.

2017. 'Reflections on Indigeneity and Religion'. In *Religious Categories and the Construction of the Indigenous* (eds. C. Hartney and D. Tower), pp. 8–37. Leiden.

Trompf, G. W., and E. Hau'ofa. 1974. 'Mekeo Chiefs and Disputing Villagers'. *Journal of the Polynesian Society* 83: 234–236.

Turner, G. 1884. *Samoa*. London.

Turney-High, H. H. (1949) 1991. *Primitive War*. Colombia, SC.

Tuzin, D. 1974. 'Social Control and the Tambaran in the Sepik'. In *Contention and Dispute* (ed. A. L. Epstein), pp. 317–344. Canberra.

    1976. *The Ilahita Arapesh*. Berkeley.

    1980. *The Voice of the Tambaran*. Berkeley.

    1997. *The Cassowary's Revenge*. Chicago.

Tyerman, D., and G. Bennet. 1831. *Journal of Voyages and Travels* (comp. J. Montgomery), vol. 1. London.

Valeri, V. 1982. 'The Transformation of a Transformation: A Structural Essay on an Aspect of Hawaiian History'. *Social Analysis* 10: 3–41.

    1985a. *Kingship and Sacrifice* (trans. P. Wissing). Chicago.

    1985b. 'The Conqueror Becomes King'. In *Transformations of Polynesian Culture* (eds. A. Hooper and J. Huntsman), pp. 79–103. Auckland.

Vayda, A. 1974. 'Maoris and Muskets in New Zealand'. *Political Science Quarterly* 85: 560–584.

    1976. *War in Ecological Perspective*. New York.

Watts, J., et al. 2015. 'Pulotu: Database of Austronesian Beliefs and Practices'. *Plos One* 10, 9: online: https//doi.org/10.137.

Wedgwood, C. 1930. 'Some Aspects of Warfare in Melanesia'. *Oceania* 1, 1: 5–33.

Weiner, A. B. 1983. *Women of Value, Men of Renown*. Austin.

Westervelt, W. D. (1910) 2010. *Legends of Maui*. Honolulu.

White, J. P., and J. F. O'Connell. 1982. *A Prehistory of Australia, New Guinea and Sahul*. Sydney.

White, J. 1887. *The Ancient History of the Maori*, 6 vols. Wellington.

Wickler, S. 2001. *The Prehistory of Buka*. Canberra.

Wilkes, A. 2019. *Honour, Mana, and Agency in Polynesian-European Conflict*. New York.

Williams, F. E. 1930. *Orokaiva Society*. London.

(1940) 1977. *The Drama of Orokolo*. Oxford.

Williams, G. 2008. *The Death of Captain Cook*. Cambridge, MA.

Williams, J. 1837. *Narrative of Missionary Enterprises*. London.

Williams, T. 1858. *Fiji and the Fijians* (ed. G.S. Rowe), vol. 1. London.

Williams, T., and J. Calvert. 1884 edn. *Fiji and the Fijians, and Missionary Labours*, 2 vols. in one. London.

Williamson, R. W. 1939. *Essays in Polynesian Ethnology* (ed. R. W. Piddington). Cambridge.

Wirihana, R., and C. Smith. 2014. 'Historical Trauma, Healing and Well-Being in Mâori Communities'. *Mai Journal* 3, 3: 197–210.

Wittfogel, K. 1981. *Oriental Despotism*. New York.

Wright, C. 2013. *The Echo of Things*. Durham, NC.

Wurm, S. A., and S. Hattori. 1981. *Language Atlas of the Pacific Area*, 2 pts. Canberra.

Young, M. W. 1971. *Fighting with Food*. Cambridge.

1983. 'The Massim: An Introduction'. *Journal of Pacific History* 18, 1: 3–10.

Younger, S. H. 2009. 'Violence and Conflict in the Pre-Contact Caroline Islands'. *Journal of the Polynesian Society* 118, 2: 135–164.

2015. 'Violence and Warfare in Precontact Melanesia'. *Journal of Anthropology* 2: [1–14] (online: hindawi.org).

Z'graggen, J. A. 1995. *Creation by Death and Deception*. Edinburgh.

# Acknowledgements

For help in sorting out difficult questions en route, special gratitude goes to Pamela Stewart and Andrew Strathern, very much valuing their interest in my work, and also to Michael Avosa, Francis Hezel, Jadran Mimica, Patrick Gesch, Anton Ploeg and Douglas Young for always being on hand to field my questions. Others to thank for special points and investigations are Sam Alasia, Janusz Bieniek, Aletta Biersack, Lynn Cook, Kirk Huffman, Andreas Jansen, Ennio Mantovani, John D'Arcy May, George Mombi, Anton Ploeg, John Shaver, Jukka Siikala, Matthew Spriggs, Will Sweetman, Daniel Tower, hermit Wendy (Bartlett) and Tigger Wise. I honour the series editors Margo Kitts and James Lewis, and Beatrice Rehl of Cambridge University Press, for their encouragement and patience; and for looking after my health how crucial has been my wife, the very caring Izabella. I dedicate this small tome to two treasured dearly departed research companions: Dr Sibona Kopi, master of all things Motuan; and Dr Friedegard Tomasetti, my intrepid collaborator in the bibliographic surveying of Melanesian religions.

## Cambridge Elements ≡

# Religion and Violence

James R. Lewis
*Wuhan University*

James R. Lewis is Professor at Wuhan University, and the author and editor of a number of volumes, including *The Cambridge Companion to Religion and Terrorism*.

Margo Kitts
*Hawai'i Pacific University*

Margo Kitts edits the *Journal of Religion and Violence* and is Professor and Coordinator of Religious Studies and East-West Classical Studies at Hawai'i Pacific University in Honolulu.

ABOUT THE SERIES

Violence motivated by religious beliefs has become all too common in the years since the 9/11 attacks. Not surprisingly, interest in the topic of religion and violence has grown substantially since then. This Elements series on Religion and Violence addresses this new, frontier topic in a series of ca. fifty individual Elements. Collectively, the volumes will examine a range of topics, including violence in major world religious traditions, theories of religion and violence, holy war, witch hunting, and human sacrifice, among others.

## Cambridge Elements ≡

# Religion and Violence

Printed in the United States
by Baker & Taylor Publisher Services